P9-CBT-054

PROGRAM ANALYSIS FOR STATE AND LOCAL GOVERNMENTS

SECOND EDITION

PROGRAM ANALYSIS FOR STATE AND LOCAL GOVERNMENTS

SECOND EDITION

by Harry Hatry
Louis Blair
Donald Fisk
Wayne Kimmel

The Urban Institute

Copyright © 1987
THE URBAN INSTITUTE
2100 M Street, N.W.
Washington, D.C. 20037

Distributed by arrangement with
UPA, Inc.
4720 Boston Way
Lanham, MD 20706

Library of Congress Cataloging-in-Publication Data

Hatry, Harry et al.
Program analysis for state and local governments

      p.   cm.
  Bibliography: p.
  1. Public administration—Cost effectiveness. 2. State
governments—Cost effectiveness. 3. Local government—Cost
effectiveness. I. Hatry, Harry P.
JF1411.P76   1988
350.007′5—dc 19

87-27372

ISBN 0-87766-410-2 (casebound)
     0-87766-409-9

Printed in the United States of America
9 8 7 6 5 4 3

JF
1411
.P76
1987

BOARD OF TRUSTEES
Carla A. Hills
  Chairman
Katharine Graham
  Vice Chairman
William Gorham
  President
Andrew F. Brimmer
Theodore F. Brophy
James E. Burke
John J. Byrne
Joseph A. Califano, Jr.
Albert V. Casey
Ralph P. Davidson
John M. Deutch
George J. W. Goodman
Philip M. Hawley
Michael Kaufman
David O. Maxwell
Robert S. McNamara
Eleanor Holmes Norton
Elliot L. Richardson
William D. Ruckelshaus
David A. Stockman
Mortimer B. Zuckerman

LIFE TRUSTEES
Warren E. Buffett
William T. Coleman, Jr.
Anthony Downs
John H. Filer
Joel L. Fleishman
Eugene G. Fubini
Aileen C. Hernandez
Vernon E. Jordan, Jr.
Edward H. Levi
Bayless A. Manning
Stanley Marcus
Arjay Miller
J. Irwin Miller
Franklin D. Murphy
Lois D. Rice
Herbert E. Scarf
Charles L. Schultze
William W. Scranton
Cyrus R. Vance
James Vorenberg

THE URBAN INSTITUTE is a nonprofit policy research and educational organization established in Washington, D.C., in 1968. Its staff investigates the social and economic problems confronting the nation and government policies and programs designed to alleviate such problems. The Institute disseminates significant findings of its research through the publications program of its Press. The Institute has two goals for work in each of its research areas: to help shape thinking about societal problems and efforts to solve them, and to improve government decisions and performance by providing better information and analytic tools.

Through work that ranges from broad conceptual studies to administrative and technical assistance, Institute researchers contribute to the stock of knowledge available to public officials and to private individuals and groups concerned with formulating and implementing more efficient and effective government policy.

Conclusions or opinions expressed in Institute publications are those of the authors and do not necessarily reflect the views of other staff members, officers or trustees of the Institute, advisory groups, or any organizations that provide financial support to the Institute.

Contents

Exhibits

Foreword

State and local government officials are continually faced with proposals for new or revamped programs and services. These proposals can have substantial effects on future costs and program performance. Grappling with these proposals, however, is often akin to gazing at a crystal ball.

Often officials receive insufficient information on the options available to them, the complete costs of these options (long-run as well as short-run), and the expected effectiveness and feasibility of each option in providing quality service. The information provided frequently is highly subjective and judgmental.

Can better and more useful information be provided to public officials for their program and policy decisions, and if so, how? The first edition of this book addressed these questions in 1976; the resulting volume stimulated such interest that a decade later The Urban Institute has prepared a second edition, revised and updated. This second edition addresses the same questions. The authors develop a series of suggestions and guidelines for improving the available information and for enriching government officials' understanding of issues underlying today's proposals.

The suggestions are presented with government analysts and contractors in mind. The book also should be of considerable interest to students planning careers in the public sector. For readers who are more administratively than analytically oriented, this volume may raise their enthusiasm for quality program analysis.

Program analysis is still as much an art as a science. Because we at The Urban Institute believe that the nation and its citizens deserve the best in decision making by public administrators, we offer this volume with the hope that it will contribute to improved program analysis by informed officials.

William Gorham
President
The Urban Institute

Preface

When we began preparing this second edition of *Program Analysis for State and Local Governments*, we expected that after ten years we might have to start from scratch. To our surprise, we found that much of the material in the first edition still applies after a decade. The state-of-the-art of program analysis has not changed substantially, but then perhaps one should not expect basic principles to change. Certainly the technology for processing data and making calculations has advanced tremendously in the past ten years. Almost every analyst now has ready access to powerful data processing programs. Computers make the collection and analysis of data considerably more feasible—and this is an important advance. Governments now have much weaker excuses for not seeking needed data.

But the key problem remains: "garbage in, garbage out." We need reliable data on costs and program effectiveness, and good thinking to ensure that these data are collected and analyzed in the right way.

The single greatest change in this second edition is the inclusion of chapter 8. We believe that program analysis needs to be related to three particular activities that state and local governments frequently address. First, governments regularly have to make choices about actions for maintaining and expanding their infrastructure, their capital facilities such as roads, bridges, water and sewer facilities, and public buildings. Second, some governments regularly review their programs for possible improvement in productivity and efficiency—and if they do not, they should. (Governments may refer to these efforts as management analyses, productivity improvement efforts, and so forth.) Third, in recent years many public agencies have begun to consider ways in which greater use can be made of the private sector; contracting is the example most often employed. Too often decisions on such moves are made without systematically considering a full range of the available options and the implications of each option on service quality and cost. Chapter 8 relates program analysis to each of these topics.

We found the program analysis case studies presented in the appendix still timely. These particular examples provide good illustrations of many program analysis principles, and we were not able to find better ones.

We have made numerous other, smaller changes. We have updated the references and tried to include many excellent materials written in the past several years.

The reader looking for a detailed, step-by-step "how-to-do-it" book will not find it here. We believe, however, that the material presented will provide insights and at least a few suggestions for improving state and local government program analysis. We hope that this work will encourage analysts to take steps to improve the methodology of program analysis.

We hope our readers will find this new edition to be timely and useful.

Acknowledgments

The authors wish to express their appreciation to a number of persons who provided valuable materials, comments, and suggestions at various stages of this work: George Barbour and Edward Everett, City of Palo Alto, California; James Cavenaugh, State of Pennsylvania; Thomas Finnie, Charlotte, North Carolina; Donald Gross, George Washington University, Washington, D.C.; Gloria Grizzle, Florida State University; Allen Holmes, Maryland Department of Budget and Fiscal Planning; Kenneth Kraemer, University of California, Irvine; Wayne Masterman, Council of State Governments, Lexington, Kentucky; Howard McMahon, Oklahoma City, Oklahoma; Fred Patrick, City of Ventura, California; Robert Sivert, Maryland Department of General Services; Richard Slocum, Metropolitan Dade County, Florida; Kenneth Voytek, Michigan Department of Commerce; Hall Tennis, Michael Gruber, and William Talbert of Metropolitan Dade County, Florida; Christopher Tomasides, City-County of Denver, Colorado; and Erwin Hargrove, Mark Fall, John Hall, Ted Miller, and Phil Schaenman of The Urban Institute.

The research forming the basis for this publication was funded by the U.S. Department of Housing and Urban Development, Office of Policy Development Research, and the Ford Foundation.

About the Authors

Harry P. Hatry has been director of the program entitled The Urban Institute and Local Government for the past fifteen years. He has worked with many state and local agencies and undertaken numerous program analysis and evaluation activities. He is the principal author of the companion volume, *Practical Program Evaluation for State and Local Governments*.

Louis H. Blair is a consultant on government policy analysis. He was on the staff of the President's Science and Technology Advisor and was formerly on the research staff of The Urban Institute. He also served during the 1970s as mayor of the City of Falls Church, Virginia.

Donald M. Fisk is an economist who heads the Bureau of Labor Statistics work on productivity measurement of government services. He has served as director of program evaluation for the County of San Diego and has conducted research for both The Urban Institute and The Rand Corporation.

Wayne A. Kimmel, a private human resources management consultant in Potomac, Maryland, has ten years of experience in the U.S. Department of Health, Education, and Welfare, five years in policy and management research, and ten years in program planning, analysis, and evaluation. He has worked in thirty-nine states and several foreign countries and has written on program performance measurement, program evaluation, needs assessment, and other human service topics.

Chapter 1
Program Analysis:
What It's All About

Executive and legislative officials in government have to make difficult decisions about how to use limited resources to meet the needs of the people the government serves. Throughout the year, but particularly at budget time, they have to decide whether to continue an existing program or to adopt new proposals or some alternative to an existing program. Short of guesswork or relying on "the way things have always been done," how should government officials decide?

There has always been an acute shortage of crystal balls, but a more systematic approach to program analysis can help. Program analysis is, in its simplest terms, the systematic, explicit examination of alternative ways to reach public objectives. The process takes in the steps of estimating the future costs, effectiveness, and other significant impacts of each alternative.

This volume indicates to state and local government personnel how program analysis might help them and describes steps for conducting useful analyses. It concentrates on the types of analysis that a state or local government is most likely to need and will have the capability to undertake. It does not delve into highly technical approaches to analysis. There are many good textbooks on technical procedures, but few basic guides written for state and local government personnel on how to establish, strengthen, or use a capability for program analysis.

Some Definitions

Let us look more closely at the definition of program analysis by defining certain key terms used in this volume.

Costs consist of expenditures of money and other resources, such as manpower, facilities, and land to carry on a program. They include both operating and maintenance expenses and investment expenses, such as training personnel, constructing facilities, and acquiring land.

Effectiveness is the extent to which a program meets specific goals or objectives. The term also connotes a program's beneficial and detrimental effects on the general public, or on specific parts of that public, called "client groups."

Alternatives are different ways of accomplishing a goal or providing a service. Alternatives may differ by the type of equipment or technology used, by the processes or procedures involved, by the levels of service provided, or by combinations of these.

Techniques of analysis are typically applied to "programs," that is, to government activities or groups of activities that provide direct services to the public, such as crime control, education, health, transportation, recreation, and waste disposal. Program analysis techniques can also be used for analyzing government "support" activities, such as purchasing, finance, and personnel.

An activity related to program analysis is program evaluation. While program analysis focuses on *future* activities, program evaluation assesses the *past* performance of existing programs. The findings of program evaluations may provide important information for program analysis, which normally considers an existing program to be one of the alternatives to be examined.[1]

An Illustration of Program Analysis

Examples of the outputs of program analysis and of the steps typically taken to reach those results are presented in exhibits 1 and 2. Exhibit 1 relates to this problem: County government officials in a northeastern state were concerned about their maternal and infant care program, in part because the infant mortality rate at the county hospital was higher than the national average. They requested an analysis of the likely costs and effectiveness of alternatives for reducing infant and maternal mortality rates and infant birth defects. Exhibit 1 shows the findings for each of three alternatives examined. Exhibit 2 summarizes the steps in the analytic process, which are typical of the basic steps in any program analysis. These steps will be discussed in more detail in chapters 3 through 6.

---

1. Program evaluation is described in a companion report, Harry P. Hatry, Richard E. Winnie, and Donald M. Fisk, *Practical Program Evaluation for State and Local Governments* (Washington, D.C.: The Urban Institute, 1981).

A discussion of the history, concepts, problems, and guidelines for evaluation can be found in Wayne A. Kimmel, "Putting Program Evaluation in Perspective for State and Local Government," Human Services Monograph 1B (Project Share, Rockville, Maryland, April 1981).

Exhibit 1. ILLUSTRATIVE SUMMARY TABLE:
            MATERNAL AND INFANT CARE PROGRAM
            ANALYSIS IN A COUNTY

Evaluation Criteria	Effectiveness and Costs		
	Alternative 1: Current Program Extended	Alternative 2: Increased Prenatal Care Emphasis	Alternative 3: Increased Postnatal Care Emphasis
1. Annual maternal death rate[a]	0.40	0.36	0.40
2. Annual infant death rate[a]	47	41	47
3. Annual infant defect rate[a]	44	37	27
4. Annual cost	$1,000,000	$1,250,000	$1,200,000

Source: Adapted from Harry Hatry, "Overview of Modern Program Analysis Characteristics and Techniques" (Washington, D.C.: The Urban Institute, 1969).

a. Rates per 1,000 births.

Contents

Chapter 2 focuses on the institutional aspects of program analysis. It discusses organizing and staffing for analysis and includes suggestions for selecting issues, scheduling, and reporting findings. Chapters 3 through 7 cover technical aspects of analysis that are of primary interest to staff analysts. They may also give decision makers a better perspective on what they should expect from program analysis. Chapter 3 discusses the overall framework for an analysis and some of the first steps in analysis. Chapter 4 discusses the estimation of program costs. Chapter 5 discusses what is probably the most difficult technical issue—the estimation of effectiveness. Chapter 6 suggests that estimating how feasible an alternative is (implementation feasibility) should be considered part of the program analysis process. This aspect has received little attention in most analyses of governmental programs. Chapter 7 presents some miscellaneous technical topics, such as "needs assessment,"

Exhibit 2.   BASIC STEPS IN A PROGRAM ANALYSIS:
MATERNAL AND INFANT CARE EXAMPLE

1. *Define problem.* What should be done to reduce a high infant mortality rate—relative to the national average—that is occurring in the county hospital?

2. *Identify relevant objectives.* The primary objectives are to minimize maternal mortality and infant mortality and abnormalities.

3. *Select evaluation criteria.* The criteria selected were infant mortality, maternal mortality, infant abnormalities, and program costs.

4. *Specify client groups.* Different client groups were mothers and children. Client groups typically have different needs and are served at different levels of effectiveness. (Although this study did not break down mortality and abnormality estimates by major demographic groups, this preferably should be done, for instance, age and ethnicity/race of the mother.)

5. *Identify alternatives.* Alternative 1 extends the current program into the future. Alternative 2 has a prenatal care emphasis, including getting expectant mothers into clinics earlier, providing nutrition services, etc. Alternative 3 has a postnatal care emphasis. (The alternatives examined should be specific, potentially operational programs. For example, Alternative 2 might call for the formation of a new clinic of certain size and location, plus a specific type of campaign to publicize it.)

6. *Estimate costs of each alternative.* In Exhibit 1, annual costs could have been shown for each of the next three to five years. They might be presented as either the average annual cost or the total cost over the period.

7. *Determine effectiveness of each alternative.* As shown in Exhibit 1, none of the three alternatives is better than the others for *all* the evaluation criteria. This will happen in most program analyses. Decision makers must now make a judgment using this and other information available to them. Showing the estimated effectiveness of each alternative for each of the next several years would be desirable since the effectiveness of different alternatives might vary over time.

8. *Present findings.* Exhibit 1 is a tabular method of displaying the estimated costs and effectiveness of alternative programs. Various graphic forms as well as text also may be used. (In this simplified example, the amount and nature of the uncertainties in the effectiveness and cost estimates are not indicated but should be presented.)

the time period to be considered in an analysis, and the handling of uncertainty when estimating cost and effectiveness. Chapter 8 discusses three major basic applications for state and local government program analyses.

Appendix A presents summaries of three actual program analyses, pointing out some of the problems likely to be encountered in a "real world" situation. Appendix B presents an outline for an "issue paper," suggested in chapter 2 as a means to begin the analysis process. Appendix C presents a checklist for assessing a program analysis.

Chapter 2
Putting Program Analysis to Work: Institutional Issues

Some of the most sophisticated and technically competent program analyses are unused and unusable. The reasons are varied: the main findings of the analysis may have vanished in a thicket of technical jargon; the recommended alternatives may be politically infeasible; the report on the analysis may have come too late; or the bureaucracy that must use the findings may be uninterested or resistant. In brief, program analysis can be elegant but irrelevant.

To avoid this danger, both the analyst and the public officials who are to use the results of the analysis must pay attention to institutional issues dealing with the ways in which studies are initiated, managed, reviewed, and used. These issues range from the way topics are selected for study to the organization of the analytic staff.

We will start with a fundamental issue: the role of the officials who request a program analysis and who will be primary users of its findings. The comments in this chapter apply primarily to executive officials, both chief executives and department heads, but many should also be of interest to legislative officials.

Role of the Executive and Staff in Program Analysis

High ranking and key officials are the people who make decisions. They choose among policy and program alternatives that consume scarce resources both immediately and in the future. These decision makers have a vital interest in getting timely, relevant, and reliable information on the costs and consequences of major decisions. This is what program analyses can help provide.

Of course, these officials will not have time to get involved in the details of the analytic process. But they can take steps that contribute to the success of program analysis. The steps are listed in exhibit 3 and are discussed here. Officials should:

1. *Participate actively in the selection of program and policy issues for analysis.* There is no substitute for the perspective which a chief executive can bring to the selection of program and policy issues. At a minimum, the executive can usefully screen lists of candidates for analysis to eliminate studies of issues which are considered to be trivial or peripheral, and to help ensure that policy questions of greatest concern are considered.

2. *Assign responsibility for the analysis to a unit of the organization that can conduct the study objectively.* If a program analysis cannot be undertaken with reasonable objectivity by the operating agency that will deliver the service, responsibility should be placed in a central staff office or with a multi-agency study team.

3. *Ensure that participation and cooperation are obtained from relevant agencies.* Even when the analysis is assigned to a central unit, staff members of agencies concerned with the issue can contribute significantly to the analysis, and their participation should be obtained whenever possible. Furthermore, their participation can help overcome some of the difficulties associated with implementing a particular alternative. The chief executive can assist an analysis by helping obtain the cooperation of these agencies.

4. *Provide adequate staff to meet a timely reporting schedule.* The effort should be staffed with enough competent people who are allowed sufficient time so that the analysis can be completed and reviewed before a decision has to be made. The chief executive should discourage the diversion of staff who are undertaking analyses to day-to-day "firefighting."

5. *Insist that the objectives, evaluation criteria, client groups, and program alternatives considered in the analysis include those of prime importance.* The executive should review the study plan early to ensure that it includes these major factors. (The selection of objectives, evaluation criteria, client groups, and alternatives is discussed in chapter 3.)

6. *Have a work schedule prepared and periodically monitored.* This ensures that interim and final study findings are available in a timely way for key decisions. A member of the executive's staff should be assigned responsibility for monitoring the effort.

7. *Review results, and if findings seem valid, see that they are used.* This helps ensure the program analysis is taken seriously within the organi-

Exhibit 3.   ROLE OF CHIEF EXECUTIVE
IN PROGRAM ANALYSIS

1. Participate actively in the selection of program and policy issues for analysis.

2. Assign responsibility for the analysis to a unit of the organization that can conduct the study objectively.

3. Ensure that participation and cooperation are obtained from relevant agencies.

4. Provide adequate staff to meet a timely reporting schedule.

5. Insist that the objectives, evaluation criteria, client groups, and program alternatives considered in the analysis include those of prime importance.

6. Have a work schedule prepared and periodically monitored.

7. Review results and, if findings seem valid, see that they are used.

zation. It is wise to circulate analysis results to interested agencies to permit reviews and comments before final actions are taken.

Selecting Issues for Analysis

While analytical resources are inevitably scarce, program issues are pervasively abundant. The usual problem is not to find issues but to select those that are most important and that could be clarified significantly by systematic analysis. Some analyses will have to be done on policy problems whose importance emerges because of sudden events; these analyses cannot be scheduled in advance. But generally, waiting for issues to reach a boiling point before undertaking an analysis is likely to prohibit in-depth analysis. State governments and most medium and large local governments will find it useful to have regular, systematic processes to identify issues before they "come to a head" and to select appropriate ones for analysis.

An inexpensive tool for identifying and describing potential topics for analysis is the "issue" or "problem-definition" paper. It describes the major features of a significant problem likely to require government action in the next several months and suggests alternative actions that the government should consider—but stops short of the actual analysis. A suggested outline for an issue paper is presented in Appendix B.

The following seven criteria, summarized in exhibit 4, should help a government select issues and programs for analysis. Criteria 1 through 3 relate to the importance of an issue; criteria 4 through 7 relate to the feasibility of analysis.

Importance of an Issue

1. *Is there a decision to be made by the government? Can the analysis significantly influence the adoption of various alternatives?* In some instances, key decision makers, such as governors, mayors, city managers, agency heads, legislators, or council members, may have clearly made up their minds. Similarly, strong and controlling interest groups may have already mobilized behind or publicly committed themselves to a single course of action. In such circumstances, the results of analysis will probably have little influence on the final action. However, if there is some suspicion that a course of action has serious defects or major hidden costs and if no decision has been made, a chief executive may wish to proceed with analysis.

2. *Does the issue involve large costs or major consequences for services?* Issues that involve large outlays of resources or hold substantial consequences for the future level, quality, or distribution of public services should receive priority for analysis. Programs that are "analytically interesting" but unlikely to have substantial impact on services or budgets are usually not worthwhile topics for program analysis.

3. *Is there substantial room for improving program performance?* If a program is of major importance but there is little room for improving it, examining a program of less "importance" but with more room for improvement may have a higher payoff. Clues to the improvement needed could come from preliminary data indicating the costs or service quality compared to those of similar jurisdictions. Similarly, if many problems or complaints arise about the service, improvement would appear to be needed.

Feasibility of Analysis

4. *Can the problem be handled by program analysis?* Does it lend itself to measurement? Can reasonable estimates of effectiveness be made?

Exhibit 4.   CRITERIA FOR SELECTING ISSUES FOR
ANALYSIS

Importance of an Issue

1. Is there a decision to be made by the government? Can the analysis significantly influence the adoption of various alternatives?

2. Does the issue involve large costs or major consequences for services?

3. Is there substantial room for improving program performance?

Feasibility of Analysis

4. Can the problem be handled by program analysis?

5. Is there time for the analysis to be done before key decisions must be made?

6. Are personnel and funds available to do the analysis?

7. Do sufficient data exist to undertake the analysis, and can needed data be gathered within the time available?

---

5. *Is there time for the analysis to be done before key decisions must be made?* Program analyses completed and reported *after* officials commit themselves to a course of action can be useless. Studies should consciously be scheduled to allow time for final results and findings to be circulated, reviewed, and evaluated before a decision. It is possible to be too pessimistic about timing, however. A "late" study now may be an early one if the same issue or a comparable one arises again.

6. *Are personnel and funds available to do the analysis?* There is little point in considering analyses that require technical skills that government personnel lack and that cannot be obtained at reasonable costs. Many governments have personnel with most—if not all—necessary analytical skills to undertake a wide range of analyses. In those instances where a technical specialty such as

conducting sample surveys is required, outside assistance might be obtained from consulting firms, universities, or research organizations.

7. *Do sufficient data exist to undertake the analysis, and can needed data be gathered within the time available?* Most existing government data records have been designed for administrative, financial, and other control purposes. Few have been designed for measuring and presenting program effectiveness. Even available cost data are often not in a form usable for program cost analyses. Required data, if available at all, may have to be extracted laboriously from existing records or obtained from new sources. Before deciding whether to undertake an analysis, the data that are available should be compared to what will be required; a judgment should be made as to whether available data are adequate, or whether it will be too difficult or expensive to generate new data.

Illustrative Issues for Analysis

Exhibit 5 gives examples of issues that might be selected for analysis. Whether a specific issue contained in the list is worth analyzing depends in part on the application of the seven criteria identified above.

Staff Time Required and Number of Analyses

The amount of staff time a study will require should be assessed in advance. Many analyses can be done within three to twelve person-months, but a complex study may require considerably more effort, possibly straining a government's analytical resources. The time required for data collection is often difficult to estimate. Where data are fragmentary, special collection efforts may be necessary. Even with experienced analysts, the time for data *collection* sometimes becomes excessive, at the expense of time for data *analysis*.

How many studies might a government undertake in a given year? This depends in large part on the resources available to do analysis and on the number of "crash" analyses arising. If a government relies primarily on one or two analysts in a central staff, one or two analyses a year may be the limit. If studies are done at the agency level as well, one study a year in each major agency may be taxing, especially where there is no prior experience with program analysis. On the whole, an approach allowing sufficient time to complete assigned analyses is probably more sensible than a broadside approach that attempts more studies and crash analyses than can possibly be finished. The latter approach results in superficiality and discredits the usefulness of analysis in both the short run and the long run. Realism is a necessary antidote to the enthusiasm of those who tend to bite off more analysis than they can chew.

Locating Responsibilities for Program Analysis

There does not appear to be a single best place to locate analytical activities in the government. Variations in the development, experience, and operating style of an organization make varying arrangements appropriate. Some basic points, however, should be considered.

1. *The sole responsibility for analysis should not be put into the hands of individual operating agencies.* Agencies may be tempted to give priority consideration only to alternatives or policy actions that are in their self-interest, and which tend to continue their current ways of operation. Operating agencies may overlook effects and impacts beyond their scope of interest or responsibility. Single-agency analyses may define problems too narrowly or employ restricted alternatives and criteria. For example, a police agency might not give full consideration to the disposition of arrests; traffic control agencies might neglect the air and noise pollution spillovers of their programs; housing authorities might be more interested in enlarging the stock of community housing than maintaining what exists in a liveable condition. It is unlikely, for instance, that a single operating agency would have had adequate perspective to undertake the analysis of drug abuse treatment programs described in appendix A-3.

A unit *outside* or *above* an operating program should direct, participate in, or at least monitor analyses. In all states and in local jurisdictions with more than about 100,000 population, at least a small central staff for program analysis and the allied functions of evaluation, program planning, and research is probably desirable. A central staff can itself conduct analyses with participation from operating agencies and possibly outside consultants; stimulate, monitor, and review agency-level studies; and provide such agency studies with technical assistance. In smaller jurisdictions, where a full-time central program analysis staff may not be feasible, these functions could be carried out part-time by one or two staff members in the chief executive's office or budget office who do not have direct operating responsibilities.

In addition to a central staff, there are often analytic capabilities available at the agency level in states and in larger jurisdictions. Some units, such as police or health planning and research units, are often engaged in gathering

Exhibit 5.   ILLUSTRATIVE ISSUES FOR PROGRAM ANALYSIS

Law Enforcement

1. What is the most effective way of distributing limited police forces—by time of day, day of week, and geographical location?

2. What types of police units (foot patrolmen, one- or two-man police cars, special task forces, canine corps units, or others) should be used and in what mix?

3. What types of equipment (considering both current and new technologies) should be used for weaponry, for communications, and for transportation?

4. How can the judicial process be improved to provide more expeditious service, keep potentially dangerous persons from running loose, and at the same time protect the rights of the innocent?

5. How can criminal detention institutions be improved to maximize the probability of rehabilitation, while remaining a deterrent to further crime?

Fire Protection

1. Where should fire stations be located, and how many are needed?

2. How should firefighting units be deployed, and how large should units be?

3. What types of equipment should be used for communications, transportation, and firefighting?

4. Are there fire prevention activities, such as inspection of potential fire hazards or school educational programs, that can be used effectively?

Health and Social Services

1. What mix of treatment programs would do the most to meet the needs of the expected mix of clients?

2. What prevention programs are desirable for the groups that seem most likely to suffer particular illnesses?

3. How extensive should eligibility and quality control procedures be?

Exhibit 5. (continued)

Housing

1. To what extent can housing code enforcement programs be used to decrease the number of families living in substandard housing? Will such programs have an adverse effect on the overall supply of low-income housing in the community?

2. What is the appropriate mix of code enforcement with other housing programs to make housing in the community adequate?

3. What is the best mix of housing rehabilitation, housing maintenance, and new construction to improve the quantity and quality of housing?

Employment

1. What relative support should be given to training and employment programs which serve different client groups?

2. What should be the mix among outreach programs, training programs, job-finding and matching programs, antidiscrimination programs, and post-employment follow-up programs?

Waste

1. How should waste be collected and disposed of, given alternative visual, air, water, and pollution standards?

2. What specific equipment and routings should be used?

3. Should collection be contracted or done in-house?

Recreation and Leisure

1. What type, location, and size of recreation facilities should be provided for those desiring them?

2. How should recreation facilities be divided among summer and winter, daytime and nighttime, and indoor and outdoor activities?

3. What, and how many, special summer programs should be made available for out-of-school youths?

4. What charges, if any, should be made to users, considering such factors as differential usage and ability to pay?

and tabulating statistics. Except in the very largest cities and some state agencies, such units typically do little full-fledged program analysis or evaluation. These units can serve, nonetheless, as the nucleus for building an agency's analytical capability. Many state governments have analysis and/or evaluation staffs in some of their larger agencies.

2. *Analysts should have access and be exposed to the needs and policy views of key decision makers.* The staffs performing analyses should probably report directly to the chief executive, department head, or to a principal advisor. Analyses are then more likely to reflect managerial and political realities.

3. *The time spent by analysts on daily "firefighting" operations should be limited.* The demands for responses to daily issues are unending and can inhibit or even prevent in-depth examination of issues. Analysts should be in touch with the dynamics of policy making, but should not be swamped with daily rush jobs.

4. *Analysis units should maintain a close relationship with budget offices.* Budget offices often have a strong voice in implementing the results of analyses. And experienced budget examiners may be very knowledgeable about program operations. Some governments have tried to make budget examiners into part-time program analysts or to give new program analysts some regular budgetary responsibilities. While appealing in principle, this arrangement sometimes creates difficulties, at least initially, because the routine burdens of budget administration require so much time.

Analysts and the budget staff can, of course, interact during the course of a study. Budget staff members can, for example, advise the analysis team on costs of alternatives. It may be possible to merge the budget staff with the analysis staff once a tradition of analysis has been established and accepted. But experience suggests that at least initially the program analysis staff should be separate.

5. *The functions of program evaluation and program analysis can and probably should be placed in the same office.* Program evaluation—the assessment of how existing programs have performed in the past—provides basic information for program analysis. Past performance can be projected into the future as part of the task of assessing alternatives. Similar skills are likely to be needed for the two functions. It may be economical to combine the two in an "Office of Program Evaluation and Analysis." But care should be taken to avoid the pressures to evaluate a program favorably because it resulted from a previous analysis conducted by the same office.

A Special Note: Use Agency Staff in the Analysis

Staff members of operating agencies concerned with the issue being analyzed are likely to be experts in their fields. Analysts who are not already familiar with the field should draw on their expertise. The agency experts should be members of an analysis "team," in cases where a team is used. Participation of experienced staff members from operating agencies and their contact with analysts will not only yield more complete, reliable, and relevant information, but will also increase the likelihood that the agency will cooperate in implementing the recommendations that result from the study.

Staff Skills and Training

To perform most analyses, an individual does not need extensive training in a major professional speciality. What an analyst needs is intelligence and an inquiring, systematic, analytical approach to solving problems. Many governments already employ staff members who successfully undertake program and policy analyses. Other staff members could qualify with training and experience.

Quantitative training in such fields as economics, engineering, or operations research gives some advantage to potential analysts because several of the premises (for example, the widespread scarcity of resources), approaches (such as routinely considering alternatives), and techniques (for instance, use of quantitative data) associated with program analysis are familiar to persons with these disciplines. But high-quality analytical work can be performed by staff members without these specialized backgrounds.

Use of Outside Resources

Analytical projects sometimes require special skills and personnel resources that are not available within a government. This is likely to occur where the analysis staff is small or when the analysis requires an "exotic" skill or speciality. Services of consulting firms, universities, and research organizations can be hired to augment existing skills.

Accessible, and sometimes inexpensive, technical resources for state and local governments often exist in nearby colleges and universities. Users should be alert, however, that some academics prefer to work on federal-level problems, may be inclined toward ivory tower solutions, or may emphasize work that is publishable from a disciplinary perspective rather than being useful for the government.

Federal government agencies, business firms, and even private civic groups such as the local League of Women Voters and chamber of commerce are sometimes potential sources of help. Both profit-making and nonprofit firms may be willing to participate in an analysis as a public service, for the sake of the learning experience, to test out or share some of their own technology, or simply to make contacts for possible future business.

Here are some examples of cooperation from outside organizations:

• As part of a cooperative effort with the city of East Lansing, Michigan, the National Bureau of Standards (NBS) loaned two technical staffers to work on an analysis of the location of new fire stations. The analysts used a component of an existing computer model which had been developed by NBS. The Bureau experts participated in a productive user-technician dialogue with city officials. Based on the success of the computer model, the city planned to use it in the analysis of several other city problems to which it appears applicable.[1]

• New York City undertook a study of the effectiveness of emergency ambulance services. Shortly after the study began, a large computer firm undertook development of a computer simulation of ambulance services. The model was used in the analysis to calculate "response times" for three alternative modes of deploying ambulances. The firm did not charge the city for the use of the model. The analyst who developed it later joined the analysis staff of the city.[2]

• The Leagues of Women Voters of both Arlington County, Virginia and Randolph Township, New Jersey have provided volunteer interviewers to their local governments for surveys of citizen experience with local government services. Similarly, the Birmingham, Alabama Health and Welfare (community services) Council assisted the city with a survey of citizen views of recreation needs and performance.

In addition to obtaining assistance with part of an analysis, a government may use an outside group, such as a consulting firm, to conduct an entire

---

1. Marvin R. Burt, Donald M. Fisk, and Harry P. Hatry, "Factors Affecting the Impact of Urban Policy Analysis: Ten Case Histories," Working Paper 201-3 (Washington, D.C.: The Urban Institute, July 1972), pp. 20–21.

2. Ibid., pp. 56–63.

program analysis. This may be required when internal staff resources are already committed, when the analysis is beyond their capability, or when a firm might bring greater "credibility" or "impartiality" to a controversial study. In these instances, governments ought to keep in mind four caveats:

1. Study costs are likely to be higher than those of an analysis conducted internally.

2. An outside group may not have or be able to acquire in the available time an adequate perspective of a complex policy problem.

3. An outside firm may be perceived as a greater threat than an internal group and perhaps find less cooperation, though in some instances the reverse may be true.

4. Implementing outside findings may not be as palatable to those inside who have to live with the consequences of recommendations which were "invented" elsewhere. Thus, although outside studies may be of higher technical quality, they may present problems when the time comes to implement their recommendations.

To improve the quality and usefulness of analyses conducted from outside, the following may be helpful:

1. *The government should be as clear as possible about what problem or problems it is asking an outside group to study.* While most problems are clarified and sometimes transformed in the very course of analysis, many studies miss their mark—and disappoint their clients—because the government really had no idea what it wanted in the first place.

2. *Before much effort has been expended, the government should review and discuss the plan to be followed with the contractor.* This includes defining and reaching an understanding of the issues or problems to be addressed, listing the major alternatives to be examined, identifying the principal criteria of effectiveness to be employed, specifying the target populations to be considered, and defining the general scope and methodology to be employed.

3. *Periodic and intensive meetings should be held during the study, especially in the early stages, to ensure communication on the subject and progress of the analysis.* A government project monitor should be assigned to each study contract.

4. *The government should specify the type and amount of staff assistance and data it will provide.* It should ensure that the contractor has reasonable

and effective access to the agencies and personnel from which information is to be obtained.

5. *The government should offer a clear understanding of the products it wants, including interim and final reports, and the schedule on which the products are to be delivered.* Findings which are too late for use in decisions are often useless. Regular written progress reports are valuable to both parties. Final reports should be in writing and accompanied by oral briefings and interpretations. The major assumptions and procedures of the study as well as the findings should be explicitly stated and documented. The data used in the study should be provided to the government in an understandable form.

Presentation of Results

If the specific findings and implications of an analysis cannot be readily understood they are not likely to be used. Even the best analysis will be ignored or rejected if it appears to be esoteric, sloppy, rambling, or incoherent. Analysts have to communicate their findings clearly to decision makers interested in very specific matters. Some decision makers prefer oral presentations; others prefer written reports. Either way, most public officials lack the time or specialized training to pore over lengthy technical arguments, long tables, computer printouts, or formulas to discover what an analysis has found. The analysts' job is to present their findings in a comprehensible way—in clear English and in a compact and orderly fashion.

Some guidelines that can make an analysis more comprehensible and meaningful are:

1. *Before distributing an analysis, have it critically reviewed.* A review of the draft by program people and one or two good technicians not involved in the analysis may turn up important ambiguities, omissions, errors, misinterpretations of data, faulty methods, bad logic, or unsubstantiated conclusions. The review can also reveal important points of debate or controversy. It is often reasonable to discuss major objections and responses to the report's recommendations in the report itself.

2. *Present findings in writing.* This will reduce the possibility of misunderstanding and permit an analysis to be reviewed. Even though decision makers may not want to read the report or have time to do so, the document should be available for staff review.

3. *Present a compact, clear summary.* The technical details of a study may thrill an analyst but bore a busy official. These details should be included

in the body of a report or in appendices, but no reader should have to wade through minutiae to reach the findings.

4. *Acknowledge the limitations and assumptions of a study.* State them explicitly. Do not force a decision maker to sniff them out. For objective analysis, the presentation should include all sides of the story: the good, the bad, and the unknown. For example, in the case of the Fort Worth car plan analysis (see appendix A-2), the city attorney indicated that he felt that the plan violated the state constitution. This was reported in the analysis but it was also pointed out that at least two other cities in the state had already started to use a similar plan.

5. *Use simple graphics where possible to communicate major findings and conclusions.* A "picture"—if it is a good one—is still worth a thousand words. Exhibit 25 in chapter 8 provides an example of the use of a bar chart to summarize the findings of one particular analysis. Other, more quantitative, examples can be seen in the tables included in appendix A that summarize the quantitative findings.

6. *Get rid of jargon.* Have one or two laymen read the body of the study to see if it is understandable.[3]

7. *Tailor the presentation to the decision maker who will use it.* Some may prefer tables, others graphs. Some will demand one-page executive summaries. Others will want to have all the details. Some will want special oral briefings, others will not.

Cost of Program Analysis

Program analysis is not free. Costs of individual studies vary widely, depending on such factors as the length of the study, the complexity of the issue, the size of the analytical team employed, the cost of data collection, and charges for outside help. Major program analyses, such as those at the federal level, have cost several hundred thousand dollars. Analyses for state and local governments, of the type discussed in this report, are likely to average three to twelve person-months of analytical effort. Extended studies may require two to three person-years.

---

3. Useful books to help technical writers write clearly are Rudolf Flesch, *The Art of Readable Writing* (New York: Harper and Row, 1949); Robert Gunning, *The Technique of Clear Writing* (New York: McGraw-Hill, 1968).

One way to put the costs of program analyses into perspective is to relate them to the costs associated with the programs under study. The federal government has earmarked anywhere from 0.5 to 2.0 percent of total program costs for analysis and evaluation. This is well above the amount currently being spent by most state and local governments.

Here are a few illustrations of the variations of costs or analysts' time spent in conducting several program analyses:[4]

• A study of the size and deployment of the fireboat fleet of a large eastern city took an analyst three weeks plus an undetermined amount of time for data collection by the fire department. The potential costs associated with the policy issue under study ranged from $500,000 to $1.5 million.

• An analysis of the need for and location of two new fire stations cost approximately $20,000 including direct city costs, outside technical assistance, and computer costs. The issue under study was whether to spend $500,000 in new capital and $130,000 in new annual operating costs to build two new fire stations.

• A senior analyst spent four months analyzing alternative ways of improving onsite trash incineration to meet minimum legal air pollution standards. The alternatives under study entailed a combined cost to the city and landlords ranging from $56 million to $404 million.

• An assessment of alternatives for reducing response times of emergency ambulance services in a large city took about one person-year and cost the city more than $100,000. The additional cost of developing and running a computer model was absorbed by an information systems firm.

• The analysis of Dade County library staffing described in chapter 8 required approximately four staff-years of analyst time over about ten months of time (the product included detailed staffing and scheduling recommendations for each of Dade County's twenty-five libraries).

• The analysis of options involving greater use of the private sector by seven State of Delaware and Maryland operating agencies (discussed in chapter 8) required from three to twelve staff-months to complete.

---

4. Marvin R. Burt, Donald M. Fisk, and Harry P. Hatry, "Factors Affecting the Impact of Urban Policy Analysis: Ten Case Histories," Working Paper 201-3 (Washington, D.C.: The Urban Institute, July 1972); and International City Management Association, "Applying Systems Analysis in Local Government: Three Case Studies" (Washington, D.C., 1972).

Whether a study is worth it is a relative consideration; there are no absolute rules. Program analyses can result not only in cost savings but also improvements in program effectiveness and public services. The latter may far outweigh in importance the direct budgetary costs of a study.

Factors Affecting the Impact of Analysis

Why do some program analyses appear to have substantial impact on the decisions of public officials, while others have very little or are ignored? A number of factors beyond a study's technical sophistication affect its impact. There is no systematic evidence to pinpoint all of them, but a review by The Urban Institute of ten case studies tells us about some of the apparent hallmarks of study success, failure, and impact on policy.[5] The studies examined are listed in exhibit 6. Ten factors were examined as to their influence on the impact of each analysis. These factors are listed in exhibit 7.

Three of the five "technical" factors examined appeared to have the strongest relationships to impact. The analyses that influenced decisions were those that:

1. Were well-timed, so that study findings were available at key decision points.

2. Included an explicit consideration of political and administrative issues that might affect the implementation of study findings.

3. Focused on well-defined problems rather than on broad or open-ended ones.

The size of the study and the adequacy of its methods seemed to be less clearly related to the study's impact.

Two of the "bureaucratic" variables examined appeared to have strong relationships to impact. The analyses which affected policy dealt with issues which could not be deferred by policy makers and focused on issues in which decision makers had shown clear interest. Whether an analysis proposed changes in a program's funding level and whether agency members who would have to implement study recommendations actually participated in the study

---

5. The material in the remainder of this section is based on Burt et al., "Factors Affecting the Impact of Urban Policy Analysis."

Exhibit 6. TEN CASE HISTORIES

1. *Fireboat A* examined the existing fireboats and various alternatives as to their type, number, and location for controlling fires near or on the waterfront.

2. *Fireboat B* examined the desirable number and location of fireboats for controlling fires on or near the waterfront.

3. *Fire Station Location* examined the question of how many fire stations there should be and where they should be located to provide fire protection.

4. *Emergency Ambulance Service* examined the number and location of ambulances needed to provide the fastest response to emergency calls.

5. *Mechanical Street Sweeping* examined the best way to allocate existing mechanical sweeping resources to maximize their effectiveness—with limited augmentation of resources as a possible option.

6. *Onsite Incineration* examined various ways of meeting new minimum air pollution standards regarding incinerators in both public and private apartment buildings, including enforcement of penalties to require upgrading of incinerators and the consequences to hauling requirements where incinerators were shut down.

7. *Solid Waste Collection and Disposal* examined a wide spectrum of collection and disposal options, including curbside versus backyard collection, various alternatives for solid waste containers, and a sanitary landfill versus incineration for solid waste disposal.

8. *Swimming Opportunities* examined various alternatives for providing swimming opportunities for the residents of a Model Cities neighborhood, including various numbers and sizes of pools and busing to a nearby ocean-front beach.

9. *Subemployment* examined how unemployment and underemployment might be reduced in the city's Model Cities neighborhood. The emphasis was on determining the effectiveness of existing manpower training programs and placement agencies.

10. *Venereal Disease Control* examined the problem of reducing the prevalence of gonorrhea and syphilis, with emphasis on gonorrhea.

Source: Burt et al., "Factors Affecting the Impact of Urban Policy Analysis."

Exhibit 7.   FACTORS EXAMINED FOR THEIR INFLUENCE
ON THE IMPACT OF ANALYSIS

Technical Variables

    1. Study size

    2. Study timing

    3. Methodological adequacy

    4. Consideration of implementation

    5. Nature of problem studied

Bureaucratic and Political Variables

    6. Decision maker interest

    7. Implementer's participation

    8. Single-agency issue

    9. Proposed changes in funding

    10. Immediate decision needed.

Source: Burt et al., "Factors Affecting the Impact of Urban Policy Analysis."

did not seem to be related significantly to the impact of analysis in these cases.

Some of the findings of this study tend to support intuitive feelings. For example, it is common sense that a study will have more impact if it is well timed, holds a decision maker's interest, and takes into account the administrative and political feasibility of implementing recommendations.

Effects of Limited Time and Resources: "Quickie" Analysis

There will be many times in state and local governments when a program analysis is needed but time and staffing to undertake it are limited. Unfortunately, the "quickie" or "crash" analysis may be the most common method for most governments. Under these circumstances, it will probably be necessary to limit the number of alternatives considered; to use data that are currently, or at least quickly, available; and to do a less comprehensive and thorough analysis.

Of course, any such shortcuts will weaken the analysis, and this should be specifically noted in the analysis report. But even "quickie" studies should apply the basic analytical principles and tools discussed in chapters 3 through 7. Limited time and resources are no excuse for neglecting the basics.

After the Analysis: Implementation and Follow-up

Analysis helps bring policy makers *to* decisions. But what should be done *after* a decision is made to implement a new program or modify an old one? Executives and analysts should consider the following approaches:

1. The executive might assign responsibility for following the implementation process to staff members (perhaps even the program analysis staff). This staff should develop a schedule for implementation, monitor the progress, and report if the process breaks down. Should problems arise or delays occur, early detection helps ensure that accountability for implementing changes is established.

2. An evaluation of an implemented program might be conducted after it has been in operation for a reasonable amount of time—both to gather information to help with future decisions and to gain feedback about the accuracy of projections analysts made. This can help analysts make improvements in their analyses. It is also a way to hold program analysts accountable for their work and to assess the program analysis process itself.

Limitations and Dangers of Analysis

Analysis can provide a decision maker with information to use in making a difficult decision, but it rarely points to a single best alternative. The decision maker will have to weigh the trade-offs, costs, and differing effects on various client groups that the analysis identifies for each alternative. Analysis does not inherently complicate decision making; it identifies complications that already exist and attempts to provide information to help the decision maker handle them.

Both decision makers and analysts should guard against the following tendencies:

1. Concentrating on aspects of a problem that are easy to analyze while downplaying other aspects that are more difficult to analyze but are just as vital.

2. Becoming so fascinated with sophisticated mathematical techniques that time and money are drained from other considerations. Sometimes simple, commonplace techniques are perfectly adequate for gathering the necessary information. In such cases, resources given to constructing an elaborate computer-based model, for example, are wasted.

3. Delaying decisions to perform more analysis for its own sake. It may sometimes be desirable from a technical viewpoint to wait for a more definitive analysis, but this must be balanced against the urgency to make a decision.

Why Program Analysis Is Not Used More Frequently[6]

An examination by researchers at The Urban Institute in the early 1980s of thirteen local governments, encompassing over twenty different operating agencies, found few examples of in-house, systematic program analysis being used to help select infrastructure repair, rehabilitation, or maintenance projects. These operating agencies, particularly the larger ones, often have a number of professionals, including many who have considerable technical background and could potentially undertake such analyses. The reasons why agencies do not systematically examine options appear to be as follows:

• Operating agency staff are heavily involved with emergency and operational responsibilities, and usually do not have time to undertake such examinations. Contractors usually conduct the intense examinations that are done.

• Similarly, funds for such activities are very limited in local governments. And because of the technical limitations to be noted later, resources for analysis are not believed to be a high priority.

---

6. The material in this section is adapted from Harry P. Hatry and Bruce G. Steinthal, *Guide to Selecting Maintenance Strategies for Capital Facilities* (Washington, D.C.: The Urban Institute, 1984), especially pages 72 and 73.

• The data needed to make comprehensive analyses—for example, information on each facility's physical characteristics and condition—are unavailable in most operating agencies.

• The analytical tools for using such data to undertake analyses of options have substantial weaknesses, in part because the agencies have had little experience with such tools and thus have not adapted them to their needs.

• Those parts of the analysis that require projections of the future have innate weaknesses, as do any attempts to forecast the future (including stock-market projections or projections of the economy for even several months, let alone one or more years, into the future).

• Operating agency personnel, particularly at the top level, are unaccustomed to such analysis and do not perceive its use and utility.

• Higher-level officials, both chief executive officers and other elected officials, have not insisted on the information for which the analyses are needed and are inexperienced in how the information obtained might be used, for example, to gain public support for proposals.

• Even when such analyses are undertaken and are subsequently transmitted for central review, the information may not be presented clearly and concisely so that central review officials can understand the material and its implications.

Some of these problems are inherent obstacles. Many, however, can be reduced, even if only gradually. For example, data on facility condition can be obtained, the various analytical tools such as those discussed in this report can be tried and refined, and improvements can be made in the communications between operating agencies, central review personnel, and elected officials.

The remaining chapters seek to help public personnel reduce these obstacles.

Chapter 3
Improving on Crystal Ball Gazing: The Basic Elements of Program Analysis

Thus far we have emphasized the roles and responsibilities of decision makers in carrying out successful program analyses. Even with the support of decision makers, program analysis is still fraught with difficulties. The remaining chapters are devoted to aiding the analyst in conducting the basic steps of program analysis. Exhibit 2 listed typical steps. While the elements are presented as a series of steps, actual analysis usually involves an interplay among the steps, such as backtracking to refine or redefine the problem, to specify additional client groups, or to pose additional evaluation criteria.

This chapter discusses the first five steps: defining the problem, identifying objectives, selecting evaluation criteria, specifying client groups, and identifying alternatives. In considering the suggestions in chapters 3 through 7, it may be helpful to refer to the three examples of analyses summarized in appendix A, and the checklist of technical criteria for assessing program analyses in appendix C.[1]

---

1. For more details on various technical procedures for program analysis see such works as Hugh J. Miser and Edward S. Quade, editors, *Handbook of Systems Analysis* (New York: North-Holland, 1985); Giandomenico Majone and Edward S. Quade, editors, *Pitfalls of Analysis* (New York: John Wiley & Sons, 1980); Theodore H. Poister, *Public Program Analysis: Applied Research Methods* (Baltimore, Maryland: University Park Press, 1978); Edith Stokey and Richard Zeckhauser, *A Primer for Policy Analysis* (New York: W.W. Norton and Company, 1978); Mathew B. Miles and A. Michael Huberman, *Qualitative Data Analysis* (Beverly Hills, California: Sage Publications, 1984); John J. Clark, Thomas J. Hindelany, and Robert E. Pritchard, *Capital Budgeting* (Englewood Cliffs, New Jersey: Prentice-Hall, 1979); and Shlomo Reutlinger, *Techniques for Project Appraisal under Uncertainty* (Baltimore, Maryland: published for The World Bank by the Johns Hopkins University Press, 1970).

Defining the Problem and Its Scope

Program analysis starts with an issue or problem. The following examples from appendix A illustrate the nature of problems as they were initially posed:

1. Nashville mayor's office: Do we need to build three new cottages at our Children's Home as proposed?

2. Fort Worth City Council: *Parade Magazine* says that Indianapolis lets their police officers drive their patrol cars while off duty, and as a result the crime rate has dropped substantially. Should we do the same?

3. Dade County manager: What drug treatment program should the county encourage and support?

An analyst should, of course, respond to a problem or issue as it is initially perceived by government officials. But beyond that, analysts should attempt to identify the "real" problem which may underlie a given issue. As initially posed, a problem may be stated vaguely, incompletely, or perhaps misleadingly. Analysts will neglect part of their job if they indiscriminately accept the characterization of a problem as it is first presented. But problems and issues should not be redefined or reformulated merely to suit the analyst or to fit his analytic tools. Significant changes in problem statements should be worked out with, or reviewed by, responsible officials before the study is well under way.

One of the first problems that an analyst will normally face is determining the scope of an analysis. Should it focus on very narrow aspects of a problem or should it encompass numerous and broad dimensions? The analysis of the Fort Worth take-home police car plan, for example, focused on a very narrow issue. It considered only the existing use of police cars in Fort Worth and the variations of the basic take-home plan used in Indianapolis. The analysts might have explored other possible ways to reduce crimes, such as providing additional police officers or improving street lighting. The analysis could also have included additional options such as one-officer versus two-officer patrol cars or uniformed versus nonuniformed patrol officers. It could have been expanded to include the role of courts and prisons in deterring and appre-hending criminals. The scope could have been further widened to consider the role of education, employment, and welfare in preventing crime in the first place. In fact, the scope was defined narrowly because of the specific interests of the city manager and council at the time.

The scope will be determined by such factors as the resouces and time available, the amount of information that is available or that can be developed in time, and the interests and needs of the government. But even within these limitations an analyst will usually have some flexibility in defining the scope. In practice, there is a common tendency to define a problem too narrowly. For example, an analysis of an emergency ambulance service was criticized for concentrating excessively on the response time of the ambulances. It had little to say either about provisions for medical care after arrival at the scene or hospital or about the relation of response time to health.

Conversely, an analysis may define an issue too broadly by attempting to answer all possible questions with one study that is so large and so difficult that it cannot be completed within the time and funding available. The choice of scope should be based in part on a preliminary analysis of a problem to help assess where analysts' time and effort would probably provide the largest payoff. An issue paper of the type described in chapter 2 and appendix B is one way to do this. Such preliminary analysis is seldom undertaken, but usually has a high payoff.

The initial scope of a study may be altered during the course of analysis, especially if important new insights about a problem arise. For example, the drug abuse treatment analysis summarized in appendix A-3 was broadened during the actual study to include the county jail when it became apparent that the jail was a major potential source of clients for treatment. As a general practice, the approximate scope of analysis should be defined at an early stage by the analysts and then reviewed by appropriate officials before a great deal of effort is expended.

One tool sometimes useful for gaining perspective on the scope of an issue is "diagramming" the service delivery system under study. This technique can help indicate how the elements of a system relate to each other and guide the selection of factors that should be considered in the analysis. Exhibit 8 is an illustration of one form of diagram. This exhibit shows various levels of a health treatment system. Each block represents a segment of the total population served by the system. If data are obtained on the number of cases falling into each block, the information could help identify those elements that are deficient and thus have priority for examination in a program analysis.

Identifying Program Objectives, Evaluation Criteria, and Client Groups

Three essential steps in program analysis are identifying relevant program objectives, criteria by which to evaluate the effectiveness of alternatives ("measures of effectiveness"), and the population or client groups that will be affected by the alternatives. These steps are closely related and will be

Exhibit 8.   AN ILLUSTRATION OF "DIAGRAMMING": ONE VIEW OF A HEALTH TREATMENT SYSTEM[a]

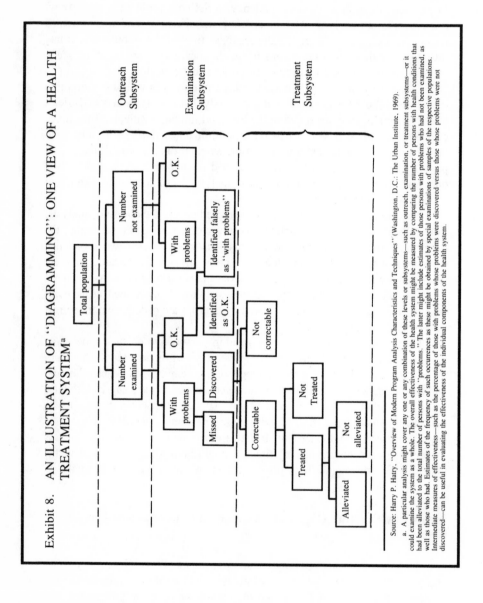

Source: Harry P. Hatry, "Overview of Modern Program Analysis Characteristics and Techniques" (Washington, D.C.: The Urban Institute, 1969).

a. A particular analysis might cover any one or any combination of these levels or subsystems—such as outreach, examination, or treatment subsystems—or it could examine the system as a whole. The overall effectiveness of the health system might be measured by comparing the number of persons with health conditions that had been alleviated to the total number of persons with "problems." The latter might include estimates of those persons with problems who had not been examined, as well as those who had. Estimates of the frequency of such occurrences as these might be obtained by special examinations of samples of the respective populations. Intermediate measures of effectiveness—such as the percentage of those with problems whose problems were discovered versus those whose problems were not discovered—can be useful in evaluating the effectiveness of the individual components of the health system.

discussed together. In practice, they can and probably should be undertaken jointly.

Whenever possible, officials who request a program analysis should review the objectives, measures, and client groups selected by the analysts before data gathering begins. This will help ensure that the coverage of the analysis is appropriate.

The terms "objectives" and "goals" refer to the purposes of a government service. An objective or goal can be a desirable result that should be maximized, or an undesirable effect that should be minimized. Some writers distinguish between goals and objectives, but we make no such distinction in this volume.

Evaluation criteria, or measures of effectiveness, are criteria that indicate the extent to which the program is achieving its objectives.

Client groups are population groups that a program is intentionally directed toward, or groups that the program unintentionally affects.

Some suggestions for carrying out these three steps of program analysis follow:

1. *Identify objectives and evaluation criteria that are people-oriented.* Objectives and the evaluation criteria associated with them should reflect potential impacts on the program's clients, usually some portion of citizens in the community. Evaluation criteria should help address the question, "How well is the service doing what it should do for the citizens who use or are affected by it?" Exhibit 9 lists some characteristics of services that such criteria should address.[2]

Ojectives and evaluation criteria should cover the public conditions that a program is designed to maintain, achieve or change. For example, criteria should measure how well a program meets the objectives of increasing the health and safety of citizens, or the cleanliness of the streets, or the satisfaction of citizens with the quality and variety of recreational opportunities.

Unfortunately, there is a widespread tendency to concentrate either on workload measures, such as tons of garbage collected, number of cases handled, or number of persons processed at intake; or on immediately available physical measures, such as number of acres of playground or number of hospital beds. While these measures may be useful for indicating some aspects of program performance, they provide little information about the extent to which citizens and the community are served effectively.

---

2. A number of candidate evaluation criteria for individual state and local government services are presented in Burt (1981), Greiner et al. (1977), Hatry et al. (1977), Millar and Millar (1981), and Schainblatt (1979).

2. *Explicitly consider potential "unintended" consequences of programs—particularly negative effects.* For example:

- Major new road building programs may result in displacement of large numbers of citizens, noise and air pollution, and disruption of the community.
- Urban renewal or housing code enforcement programs may reduce the amount of low-income housing available in a community.
- Increased arrest activities by public safety officials could, without proper safeguards, cause undue citizen harrassment.
- New solid waste disposal technology may cause objectionable amounts of air or noise pollution.

The key point here—one that is often neglected—is that an explicit objective should be to control a program's negative consequences. Objectives are usually expressed as the beneficial effects that are intended but most programs

---

Exhibit 9.   CHARACTERISTICS THAT EVALUATION
                 CRITERIA SHOULD ADDRESS

1. To what degree does the service meet its intended purposes, such as improving health, reducing crime, or increasing employment?

2. To what degree does the program have unintended adverse or beneficial impacts? For example, does a new industry increase water and air pollution or cause inconvenience to citizens?

3. Is the quantity of the service provided sufficient to meet the needs and desires of citizens? What percent of the eligible "needy" population is actually served?

4. How fast does the program respond to requests for service?

5. Do government employees treat citizens who use the service with courtesy and dignity?

6. How accessible is the service to users?

7. Do citizens who use the service, or who might use the service, view it as satisfactory?

8. How much does the program cost?

also have negative consequences. Each program alternative should be examined to assess possible side-effects, both beneficial and harmful. Explicit consideration of negative consequences will help put the overall worth of a program into proper perspective and help governments design programs that reduce negative consequences.

3. *Consider more than one objective and evaluation criterion.* Most programs have several purposes, some of which may be interdependent or even conflicting. A single objective will rarely describe adequately the effects of the program, nor will a single evaluation criterion fully measure its impact. Some of the many aspects of a program that may need to be covered by evaluation criteria were listed in exhibit 9. Exhibits 10 and 11 illustrate evaluation criteria from two program analyses summarized in appendix A.[3]

4. *Do not reject evaluation criteria because of apparent difficulties in measuring them.* Evaluation criteria should be identified without initial concern for how or whether they can be measured. There are generally ways to partially measure even qualitative, subjective criteria, for example, by estimates based on ratings by experts or on systematic surveys of former clients. In any case, analysts should identify evaluation criteria even where they can provide no information on them. This will help ensure that decision makers using an analysis will be aware of important omissions and will remember to consider those aspects that are relevant but not measured.

5. *Too many objectives or criteria are better than too few.* It is probably better to err initially on the side of including too many objectives or evaluation criteria for consideration than to eliminate some that might be important when examined more closely. Neither public officials nor program analysts should be quick to eliminate a potential evaluation criterion on the basis of their own personal opinion. Criteria that become irrelevant or insignificant during the course of an analysis can be discarded, but it is often difficult to introduce new ones midway in the process without repeating data collection efforts.

6. *Specify client groups on which the analysis should attempt to estimate program impacts.* A program usually affects different groups in different ways and to different degrees. An analysis should identify these groups and collect information on how the program will affect them. For example, the

---

3. These are not presented as examples of perfect objectives or evaluation criteria but only as reasonable ones that appeared to have been relevant, reasonably comprehensive, and useful for the analyses in which they were applied.

Exhibit 10.   ILLUSTRATION OF OBJECTIVES AND EVALUATION CRITERIA: NASHVILLE NEGLECTED AND DEPENDENT CHILDREN PROGRAM ANALYSIS[a]

Objectives

A. Reduce the number of neglected and dependent (N-D) petitions filed and the number of children subjected to the system by screening out those cases in which a petition is not justified.

B. Keep the child in his or her home or in a family environment when possible until a thorough study can be conducted and the disposition of the case is decided. Seek to avoid institutional placements.

C. Keep the child in his or her home or an appropriate environment when longer-term care is required.

D. Place all children in a stable environment to which they can adjust, where they will not become neglected again, and where they will not become delinquent.

E. Operate the system efficiently so as to minimize the costs of achieving all of the preceding objectives, or to achieve these objectives for the largest number of children when resources are constrained.

Measurement Criteria

Objective A

1. Number of N-D petitions filed.

2. Number of different children named on N-D petitions.

3. Number of cases screened where a petition was not filed.

Objective B

1. Number and percent of children kept in their own home until Juvenile Court hearing, after which they remain in their home.

Exhibit 10. (continued)

2. Number and percent of children avoiding institutionalization because of emergency caretakers.

3. Number and percent of children avoiding institutionalization because of placement in emergency foster homes.

4. Number and percent of children avoiding institutionalization because of homemakers.

Objective C

1. Number and percent of dispositions by the Juvenile Court that are considered to be good, questionable or bad as determined by professional opinion.

Objective D

1. Number and percent of children whose adjustment in placement is judged to be: satisfactory; questionable; unsatisfactory.

2. Number and percent of children moved from one placement to another.

3. Number and percent of children who develop delinquency records.

Objective E

1. Total cost of system.

2. Cost per child for each type of treatment.

Source: Adapted from Marvin R. Burt and Louis H. Blair, *Options for Improving the Care of Neglected and Dependent Children* (Washington, D.C.: The Urban Institute, March 1971).

a. See appendix A-1 for a summary of the program analysis in which these were considered.

average crime rate or unemployment rate for a jurisdiction masks differences among subgroups of a population. The following points should be considered:

- Each program will be directed toward some groups that are *intended* beneficiaries (clients) of the service.
- The program may have some impact on other groups that are *not* intended beneficiaries but are nonetheless affected beneficially or detrimentally by the program.

Exhibit 11.   ILLUSTRATION OF OBJECTIVES AND
              EVALUATION CRITERIA: FORT WORTH
              TAKE-HOME PATROL CAR PROGRAM
              ANALYSIS[a]

Objectives

To reduce the amount of crime, particularly street crime; to prevent automobile accidents and personal injuries and deaths resulting from them; to improve citizen feelings of security; to improve the public image of the police; to improve police morale; and to operate the plan as efficiently as possible to minimize the cost of achieving the preceding objectives.

Measurement Criteria

1. Number and rate of crimes of various types—especially those potentially deterrable by the presence of a police car in the vicinity, such as auto theft, robberies, and street accidents.
2. Crime clearance rates.
3. Number of traffic accidents, injuries, and fatalities.
4. Index of citizen feeling of security, such as percent of citizens feeling safe walking in the streets at night.
5. Index of police-community relations, such as citizen ratings of police responsiveness, fairness, and courtesy.
6. Index of police morale, based on survey.
7. Program costs.

Source: Adapted from Donald M. Fisk, *The Indianapolis Police Fleet Plan* (Washington, D.C.: The Urban Institute, October 1970).

a. See appendix A-2 for a summary of the program analysis in which these were considered.

- The citizens of a community or state considered as a whole often comprise a category that should be explicitly identified.
- In some cases, *future* clients (such as those who will become eligible, who will move into the city or state, or perhaps be born there) may be important groups to consider explicitly if their interests are likely to be affected by the program.

- Even internal administrative support activities (such as building maintenance, data processing, vehicle maintenance, and personnel) have
clients whose needs should be considered. The clients of these support
activities are government personnel served by those activities.

A list of typical characteristics for classifying client groups is presented
in exhibit 12. Each program is likely to be directed toward some unique client
group or groups. Examples of groups that are likely to be affected by specialized programs are presented in exhibit 13.

Analysts should try to estimate the impact of a program on different
client groups according to each of the evaluation criteria—at least those
criteria for which the impact seems likely to differ significantly among client
groups.

7. *Always include dollar costs as one criterion.* Program costs should
be estimated for each alternative. Estimating cost is discussed in chapter 4.

Sources for Identifying Relevant Objectives, Criteria, and Client Groups

It is rare to find program objectives, criteria, and client groups neatly
described and packaged. A variety of sources may provide important clues
to them:

- Legislative statements, such as ordinances, laws or resolutions sometimes discuss objectives. These are more likely to be available for state and
federally originated programs than for local ones.

- Statements made by legislators, citizen groups, or individual citizens
at public hearings discussing the program may indicate objectives. These may
have been reported in press accounts.

- Program personnel will often be aware of many intended or unintended
impacts that need to be considered as well as of population groups that are
likely to be affected.

- Government executives sometimes express program objectives and
intended beneficiaries in statements to the legislature, the press, and the
public, and in internal executive communications.

- Concerns expressed by clients of the service, perhaps obtained by an
examination of government complaint records or by interviews, may identify
service qualities of importance to them.

Exhibit 12.   TYPICAL CLIENT GROUP CLASSIFICATION
CHARACTERISTICS

1. Residence location—clients grouped by neighborhood, service area, precinct, etc., for local governments or by county, region, planning district, etc., for states.[a]

2. Sex

3. Age groups, such as youth and the elderly

4. Family income

5. Racial and ethnic groups

6. Problem or handicap groups—for example, individuals with alcohol problems or physical disabilities

7. Education level

8. Homeownership and type of dwelling

9. Employment status

10. Family size

11. Usage of particular facilities—for distinguishing among citizens with varying degrees of use of the service (including nonusers).

---

a. In addition to reflecting residential location directly, this category may be a reasonable proxy for other socioeconomic characteristics.

• Program evaluations and analyses conducted by other governments (including the federal government), academic or research institutions, and professional associations, will have identified objectives, criteria, and client groups.

Exhibit 14 contains a set of questions that might be asked by program analysts to help identify objectives, evaluation criteria, and appropriate program clients.

Exhibit 13. ILLUSTRATION OF CLIENT GROUP
CHARACTERISTICS OF SPECIALIZED
SERVICE PROGRAMS

Type of Service	Client Groups Likely To Be of Special Relevance for Program Analysis
Recreation	Individuals in different neighborhoods or regions Sex—males and females often have different recreation interests Age—the very young and elderly have special needs Individuals with handicaps Individuals without access to an automobile Low-income families Users of specific types of recreation (e.g., golf, tennis, or hiking)
Drug abuse treatment	Individuals with different lengths and types of addiction Different age, sex, income class, or racial groups Families of addicts or potential addicts Citizens as a whole, particularly as potential victims of drug-related crime
Transportation	Individuals in different neighborhoods or regions Individuals without access to an automobile (e.g., the very young, the elderly, housewives left without an automobile, or those who cannot afford or do not want to drive) Individuals with physical handicaps Low-income families Individuals with unusual working hours
Solid waste collection	Individuals in different neighborhoods Elderly and physically handicapped individuals who may require special collection services Single vs. multiple housing unit customers Residential vs. commercial customers Rural vs. urban customers

Selecting the Final Set of Effectiveness Measures

Analysts who follow the previously discussed steps will probably develop an extensive list of measures of effectiveness. The complete list may have to be narrowed to a relevant and manageable number so that data collection is not overwhelming. Some criteria for selecting a final set are shown in exhibit 15.

Exhibit 14.   QUESTIONS TO HELP IDENTIFY
                     OBJECTIVES, EVALUATION CRITERIA,
                     AND CLIENT GROUPS

1. What are the purposes of the program? Why was it (or should it be) adopted?

2. What is to be changed by the program, in both the immediate future and the long run? How would the program manager know if the program was working or not working? What would be accepted as evidence of success?

3. Who are the targets of the program? Is the community as a whole likely to be affected either directly or indirectly? Who else might be affected by the program?

4. What are possible side effects, both immediate and long-run?

5. What would be the likely consequences if the new program were introduced or if an existing program were discontinued? What would be the reaction of citizens in the community? Who would complain? Why would they complain? Who would be glad? Why?

Search for Alternatives

Central to every useful program analysis is the development of an appropriate set of alternatives that might achieve the program objectives. The following sources often help identify program alternatives:

1. If the analysis has been initiated by specific proposals by government officials, these officials may also identify alternatives they wish considered.

2. Program personnel often have specific ideas on alternatives as well as a thorough knowledge of what agencies in other governments are trying.

3. Individuals and groups outside the government, including citizens, community organizations, public interest associations, and the news media will often make proposals.

4. Approaches of other governments to the same problem should be explored. Ideas being tried by others can often be identified through profes-

Exhibit 15.   CRITERIA FOR SELECTING FINAL
SET OF MEASURES

Importance

Does the measure provide useful and important information on the program that justifies the difficulties in collecting, analyzing or presenting the data?

Validity

Does the measure address the aspect of concern? Can changes in the value of the measure be clearly interpreted as desirable or undesirable? Is there a sound, logical basis for believing that the program can have an impact on the measure?

Uniqueness

Does the information provided by the measure duplicate or overlap with information provided by another measure?

Accuracy

Are likely data sources sufficiently reliable or are there biases, exaggerations, omissions, or errors that are likely to make the measure inaccurate or misleading?

Timeliness

Can data be collected *and analyzed* in time for the decision?

Privacy and Confidentiality

Are there concerns for privacy or confidentiality that would prevent analysts from obtaining the required information?

Costs of Data Collection

Can the resource or cost requirements for data collection be met?

Completeness

Does the final set of measures cover the major concerns?

sional meetings, journals, government professional interest groups, and word of mouth.

5. Different sizes of the same alternative, such as expansions or contractions of an existing program, often need to be considered.

6. Combinations of individual alternatives may be defined as new alternatives.

7. During the analysis, new variations or new ideas may be suggested to alleviate the apparent weaknesses of basic alternatives that are found. Modifications in an alternative may be made to hedge against these weaknesses. For example, if construction of a *new* facility seems risky, an alternative might be renting facilities until key uncertainties have been reduced or eliminated. Or, a program may be adopted on a trial basis; the decision on whether to adopt the full-scale program can be made when better information is obtained.

8. It might be useful to hold "brainstorming" sessions where analysis and agency personnel and perhaps others try to generate ideas. The purpose of such sessions would be to encourage imaginative, innovative, even radically new options.

An old story, and one we cannot vouch for, concerns a fish processing plant. It brought in live fish and kept them that way until needed. To reduce costs it wanted to reduce storage space but found that when the fish were packed tightly, they became inactive and food flavor suffered. Many shapes and sizes of tanks were tried to get active movement of the fish without requiring large amounts of storage capacity. The alternative finally hit upon was to put a small sand shark in the tank. It worked wonders. It kept the fish quite active in a small area with only a small loss in fish.

9. Pilot tests of a new approach, rather than full-scale implementation, may be appropriate in some situations. This option is desirable when uncertainties about the workability and performance of a new approach are major, and when such a trial is feasible. Generally pilots are scaled-down versions of an approach. For example, the new approach might be introduced for a trial year in one part of the community, while using the existing approach elsewhere.

10. Hard, knowledgeable, and careful thinking about a problem is often a neglected source of worthwhile alternatives.

For any given set of objectives a large number of conceivable alternatives (or variations) can be proposed. As a practical matter, it is necessary to restrict the number of alternatives to be analyzed.[4] Most analyses consider no more than five or six alternatives. An analyst will have to make some early judgments, perhaps supported with preliminary, informal analysis and guidance from decision makers, to reduce a large list to a reasonable size.

Sometimes the program finally selected by government officials for implementation will *not* be among the alternatives explicitly examined in the analysis but a variation of one or more of them. This may be a result of political compromise, or because the analysis itself suggests that a new variation be generated, or it may occur because the initial alternatives are no longer appropriate.

A caution: Decision makers sometimes have preconceived ideas about which alternative is preferable. Other alternatives might then be offered that are merely "sops" to analysis—impractical alternatives or minor variations of the preferred one. For meaningful analysis, however, only alternatives that are valid options, that actually address the problem under study and represent a range of possible actions, should be included.

The degree to which a set of alternatives includes departures from existing programs will significantly affect the task of estimating the alternatives' costs and effectiveness. To provide a preliminary basis for discussing the problems of, and approaches to, making estimates of costs and effectiveness, we categorize alternatives into five types:

Type 1. Present program extended at same level of effort;
Type 2. Present program extended but at a different level of effort;
Type 3. Other variations of the present program;
Type 4. New programs with traditional concepts; and
Type 5. New programs with new concepts.

A program analysis could study alternatives from a number of these categories. An emergency ambulance study proposed four alternatives of three different types:[5]

1. Maintain the status quo (Type 1);
2. Increase the number of ambulances at the district's hospital (Type 2);
3. Redistribute the existing ambulances in the district; locate some ambulances at satellite garages (Type 3); and
4. Increase and redistribute ambulances (a combination of Types 2 and 3).

---

4. A useful discussion of ways to screen alternatives is presented in Walker (1984).
5. See Burt et al., "Factors Affecting the Impact of Urban Policy Analyses."

While there is not always a clear distinction between these five types, we will briefly examine each, especially in terms of the problem involved in estimating costs and effectiveness.

Type 1. *Present program extended at same level of effort.* The alternative most commonly considered in analyses is the existing program continued into the future with no significant change. This provides a baseline against which other alternatives can then be compared.

In this case, estimating costs is usually straightforward, at least for the near future. Many governments already project costs of current programs for at least one year as part of budget preparation; some state governments with biennial budgets make two-year projections. Where program cost projections do not exist, it is usually possible to estimate them without great difficulty. Still, quantitative estimates should be made of the effects of such factors as future inflation, pay raises, changes in workloads or caseloads, and replacement of equipment or facilities that might alter costs.

While cost of an existing program may be easy to assess, estimating its effectiveness is likely to be difficult. Few programs in state or local government have been the subject of recent program evaluation that might serve as an adequate basis for future projections of effectiveness. But with existing programs, at least crude assessments of past performance can often provide a basis for estimates of future performance. While estimates of future workload (caseload) or program demand are needed, they can often be based on past service experience.

Some external factors may change a program's effectiveness in the future and should be considered. For example, the closing of local industrial plants may change the future effectiveness of existing employment programs. Even the analysis of continuing an existing program is likely to involve more than projecting current costs and effectiveness in a straight line on the basis of past experience.

For example, in the Fort Worth take-home police car analysis, the new proposal was compared to the existing police car arrangement. Costs for the existing arrangement were projected six years into the future, a fairly simple task since there were no planned increases in the size of the force, number of patrol officers, number of police cars, or time on patrol. But it was not so easy to estimate what future effectiveness would be. As in most other jurisdictions, crime and automobile accidents were increasing; however, the analysis simply assumed that these increases would continue at recent rates.[6]

---

6. See appendix A-2 and Fort Worth Research and Budget Department, "The Use of Police Patrol Cars by Off-Duty Patrolmen" (Fort Worth, Texas, 1970).

Type 2. *Present program extended at a different level of effort.* An option commonly examined is the continuation of the same program concept but with a higher or lower level of resources. Some examples would be proposed increases in the number of motorized patrol units, reductions in the number of institutional facilities, and increases in the number of recreation facilities. Though straightforward, such actions affect both program cost and effectiveness.

Problems of estimation related to continuing the existing program apply equally to this one. There are also additional problems of estimating the costs and effects of revised program *size*. How much does it cost to add fifteen more police officers, or keep playgrounds open two additional hours per day, or train fifty additional persons? Usually, these questions cannot be answered reliably simply by using past average costs. Additional issues must be addressed: Are more facilities, equipment, or supervisory personnel also needed, and of what type? With respect to future needs for facilities or equipment, what unused capacity currently exists, and how much money can be saved by using this capacity? If a program alternative calls for a cutback, an analyst must be realistic and face up to the perennial stickiness in cutting back resources—considering vested interests within and outside the government that may effectively resist cutbacks.

Similar problems exist in estimating effectiveness. An alternative which calls for another recreational facility or a new fire station will have an impact on effectiveness, but probably at a diminishing rate compared to previous additions. There may also be unevenness or "nonlinearity" in changes in effectiveness. For example, adding a few police may have virtually no impact on effectiveness, while drastically increasing the number in an area may lead to a substantial impact.

A radical version of this type of alternative is to *eliminate* the program. On occasion, a program may have outlived its usefulness or be completely ineffective.

Type 3. *Variations in present program procedures.* This type of alternative involves a modification in the design of the existing program, not simply a change in its level of operations. For example, police might revise their preventive patrol procedures; employment agencies might modify their training programs; or the sanitation department might change from back-door to curbside pickup of garbage.

Costs and effectiveness for this type of alternative will be more difficult to estimate than for the previous types, but estimates can continue to draw on experiences with the current program.

Type 4. *New programs with traditional concepts.* Changes in current practices eventually become so great that they no longer represent mere variations of an existing program.

For example, a county's analysis of water recreational opportunities for children of low-income families considered three alternatives: (1) build six small community-size pools, (2) build three Olympic-size pools, and (3) bus children to a local beach. Neither of the latter two alternatives had been previously used by the government, but each was based on well-known elements. They could be considered alternatives of this type.[7]

This type of alternative formulation is one relatively safe way for governments to innovate. While the risks are larger than those of merely varying an existing program, they are not likely to be major. Since the proposed basic concepts often have already been tried somewhere, estimates of their costs and effectiveness can be based, at least in part, on past experiences of other governments.

Type 5. *New programs with new concepts.* This is the least common type of alternative. It presents the greatest difficulties in estimating costs and effects. The risks for a government prevent its frequent use. However, options of this type may be the best way to make major progress over the long run, either in reducing costs or in increasing effectiveness. New drugs for treating some forms of mental illness and radical new approaches to rehabilitating inmates or alcoholics would fall into this category. New concepts are often tied to new technology, but they need not be. A proposed change from delivery of a service to contracting the service to a private firm probably also belongs in this category.

The costs and effects of new programs with new concepts are particularly difficult to estimate, simply because they are "new" and thus largely untested. Whether a concept will really work at all may be unknown. Most new concepts take a long time to implement, refine, and test. By the time they are perfected, conditions may be quite different from those today. As will be noted in chapters 4 and 5, techniques used to estimate the costs and effects of new concepts may be quite different from those used to estimate more familiar program alternatives. The problems with new concepts are vividly portrayed by past attempts to introduce computer controlled traffic signals in several U.S. cities. Costs were greatly underestimated, and where the automated

---

7. See Burt et al., "Factors Affecting the Impact of Urban Policy Analysis."

signals worked, it is not obvious that the intended effects were achieved.[8] Small pilot tests of such alternatives often may be appropriate as a way to obtain better cost and effectiveness information before committing resources on full-scale programs.

---

8. See Harry P. Hatry et al., *Practical Program Evaluation for State and Local Governments* (Washington, D.C.: The Urban Institute, 1981).

Chapter 4
Estimating Program Costs

After the steps described in the previous chapter have been taken, the question becomes how much each alternative will cost. The costs and effects of each alternative should be estimated for at least one year, preferably for several years, into the future.

The type of analysis discussed here is not the same as the more common budget and cost control type of costing. The emphasis here is on estimating future program costs for a number of alternatives, not on determining what has been spent and how efficiently. Nevertheless, current cost accounting systems will be an important source of information for program cost analysis. Cost estimation for program analyses is likely to place additional demands on, rather than become a substitute for, information currently obtained by internal management cost information systems.

This chapter presents some of the major issues in estimating costs.[1] The issues are discussed in terms of three phases of cost estimation: (1) describing the alternatives in sufficient detail so that each can be costed, (2) determining which costs should be included in the analysis, and (3) estimating the costs.

---

1. For more detail see: The George Wasington University, State-Local Finances Project, "The Role and Nature of Cost Analysis in a PPB System," PPB Note 6 (Washington, D.C., June 1968); Gene H. Fisher, *Cost Considerations in Systems Analysis* (Santa Monica, California: The Rand Corporation, December 1970); Harry Hatry et al., *Efficiency Measurement for Local Government Services* (Washington, D.C.: The Urban Institute, 1979), particularly chapter 6, "Cost Estimation Issues"; Joseph T. Kelley, *Costing Government Services* (Washington, D.C.: Government Finance Research Center, 1984); and Massachusetts Executive Office of Communities and Development, *Costing and Pricing Municipal Services* (Boston, Massachusetts: Commonwealth of Massachusetts, April 1982).

Describing the Alternatives in Sufficient Detail so that Each Can Be Costed

Once the analyst has identified the alternatives to be considered in an analysis, the job is to describe each one in specific, operational terms so that estimates of cost can be made. The description should include major physical features: estimated number and type of personnel, supplies, equipment, facilities, etc. The description should also include aspects of the way the program will operate that may have a significant effect on costs and effectiveness.

How much detail is necessary to estimate costs? It is difficult to generalize. An example may help. The cost analysis of a new police helicopter program would need to develop such varied information as:

1. How often the helicopters would be used, including number of flying hours per year and for which time periods they would be needed.

2. Various characteristics of the helicopters and the plan of operation for estimating fuel, maintenance, and facility costs.

3. Various characteristics of the plan of operation for estimating the number and types of personnel and their skill levels.

4. Support requirements such as facilities and training programs.

A basic early step is to estimate how much demand there will be for the service and how many units of the various resources—such as the numbers of personnel, vehicles, and square feet of floor space—will be required to provide the service at that level. Exhibit 16 illustrates calculations for estimating the number of patrol cars needed for two alternatives of the Fort Worth take-home patrol car analysis.

The program characteristics used to estimate costs should be compatible with the characteristics used to estimate effectiveness. This may seem obvious, but it is surprisingly easy to err here, especially if program characteristics are changed frequently during the analysis. Many an analysis goes awry because it describes a special performance capability for a program alternative without counting in the added cost needed to achieve that extra capability.

In the previous example, if police helicopters are to operate at night, this will influence estimates of both cost and effectiveness. Details of night capabilities will need to be identified, such as the capability to track suspects. Cost estimates should include the added helicopter and ground equipment such as lights, as well as additional personnel and possible differential pay rates required to operate at night.

Exhibit 16.   ILLUSTRATION OF CALCULATIONS FOR
ESTIMATING RESOURCE INPUTS: NUMBERS
OF PATROL CARS NEEDED

	Alternative 1: all 289 eligible patrol officers take a car[a]	Alternative 2: 90% of all eligible patrol officers take a car[a]
Number of officers who refuse cars	0	29
Number of cars driven off duty	289	260
Extra backup cars (10%)	29	26
Total number of cars needed to support plan	318	286
Cars needed for nonparticipants in plan	0	10
Total number of patrol cars needed	318	296
Less vacation car equivalents	11	10
Total cars needed	307	286
Current cars available	102	102
Additional cars needed	205	184

Source: Fort Worth Research and Budget Department, "The Use of Police Patrol Cars by Off-Duty Patrolmen" (Fort Worth, Texas, 1970).

a. Willingness to accept a car was considered by the analysts to be an important unknown. They tested two alternative assumptions, with costs subsequently estimated for each.

In general analysts need to work closely with agency personnel to make sure that all significant cost elements and operational factors, such as training, personnel, and facility availability, are included in the analysis.

Determining What Costs Should Be Included

For the most part, program analysis will involve consideration of alternatives to existing programs. The basic problem of cost analysis is to determine the *differences* in costs among alternatives. However, the government will also need to consider *total* costs in relation to other government activities and of course to determine overall revenue requirements. The following concepts are usually involved:

1. *The cost analysis should focus on those cost elements that are likely to be substantial and that seem likely to vary significantly among the alternatives being considered.* Some cost elements will not vary significantly among the alternatives considered. For example, if all the alternatives require the same facilities and impose the same burden on existing facilities, then facility and maintenance costs would be the same and the analysis would not have to focus on them.

2. *For each alternative, analysts should determine which costs are fixed and which are variable.* For example, if a government is considering switching from one type of solid waste disposal operation to another, it is necessary to identify which of the vehicles and facilities already available can be used in the revised operation. Other costs, such as certain supervisory and facility costs, might not be affected or might be only partially affected by the change. Only those elements of cost that need to be increased or that can be decreased in the switchover from one system to the other are "variable."

In the long run no cost is actually fixed. For example, even the cost of departmental supervision is likely to increase as more and more programs are added to the department. Such increases might take the form of added staff, added facilities, or larger salaries and benefits for supervisory personnel in recognition of their increased responsibilities.

3. *The "marginal," "incremental," or "additional" costs incurred for a specific alternative are the relevant costs, not the average costs.* For example, suppose a government must decide whether to add one more swimming pool at a recreation facility or two more pools. The marginal cost of the second is how much more money it costs to build two pools than it costs to build one. Quantity discounts, for example, might reduce the unit cost of the

second pool. If one pool could be obtained for $200,000 and two for $300,000, the relevant cost of the second is $100,000, not $150,000 (the average cost of the two).

4. *"Sunk" costs, those costs which have already been spent, are irrelevant.* For example, the fact that last year the government spent $500,000 to rehabilitate a facility is not relevant to the cost analysis.[2] There may be political reasons why the government will be concerned about the previous expenditures; the analyst concerned about the feasibility of implementing an alternative (see chapter 6) needs to be aware of these reasons. Nevertheless, recommending an inferior alternative because of the past $500,000 expenditure is merely throwing good money after bad. Only the future costs of the facility, such as those for operation, maintenance, and rehabilitation, are pertinent.

5. *Costs should be considered regardless of where they are carried on the accounting books, what organizational unit they are connected with, or where the money comes from.* Exhibit 17 presents a checklist of cost elements that might apply to any type of government program. Exhibit 18 illustrates cost elements for a specific analysis.

Costs are frequently borne by more than one department, funding source, or account. A common example is vehicle maintenance performed in a centralized garage. For program analysis purposes the costs for this maintenance should be included in the costs of the programs that use the vehicles. Building maintenance is a similar example—social service programs should be charged with relevant maintenance costs for facilities.

Another case is employee benefits. These benefits, which may add 15 to 30 percent or more to personnel costs, are typically charged to a separate account. Capital costs, even though handled in other funds and in a separate budget document, also need to be included in program analyses.

The analyst should consider the future cost implications of each of the alternatives. A decision to build a facility or buy a large item of equipment in one budget year imposes future operating and maintenance costs. A federal grant that covers only certain investments such as construction costs will often entail future expenditures for maintenance. The cost analysis needs to include these obligations.

6. *Some program alternatives will generate revenues, such as bridge and highway tolls, charges to consumers for water and sewers or health*

---

2. However, if there is a potential "salvage" value, for example, for facilities, this return would be pertinent to any program alternative that includes disposal of the items.

Exhibit 17.   ILLUSTRATIVE LIST OF ELEMENTS OF
PROGRAM COST: A GENERAL CHECKLIST

I. *Investment costs*—costs which vary primarily with the size of program but not its duration.

Initial planning, development, and engineering costs.
Test and evaluation
Land
Buildings and facilities
Equipment and vehicles
Initial training

II. *Recurring costs*—("operating and maintenance" costs)—costs that vary with size and duration and are typically estimated on a per-year basis.

Personnel salaries and wages
Fringe benefits
Maintenance and repair of equipment, vehicles, and buildings
Direct contributions and payments to citizens, e.g., welfare payments to the needy
Payments to private institutions for services for citizens, for example, payments to agencies for foster home services
Miscellaneous materials and supplies
Miscellaneous support (overhead) costs
Refresher training, recruitment, and training costs of replacement employees

service, and recreation user fees. Such revenues as grants from the federal government may also be associated with particular program alternatives. The amount of these revenues, when believed to be substantial, needs to be estimated. *Relevant revenues should probably be considered either as offsets to total costs or as "side benefits."* In general, where the receipts are specifically collected in the course of program operation (such as with tolls, golf course fees, and water and sewer charges), these revenue items may be

---

Exhibit 18.   ILLUSTRATIVE COST ELEMENT LIST FOR A
POLICE HELICOPTER PROGRAM ANALYSIS

Investment costs

Planning and tests
Helicopters
Initial purchase of spare parts
Purchase of land for maintenance, storage and landing
Construction of helicopter pads, fueling, communications, and
    other operating facilities
Initial training of crews
Initial training of maintenance personnel

Recurring costs

Pay and fringe benefits of crews
Pay and fringe benefits of maintenance and other support
    personnel
Fuel and oil
Maintenance parts
Crew training—replacement crews or refresher training
Repair and maintenance of facilities
Insurance—liability and damage to helicopter and personnel
Replacement of helicopters and other major equipment

---

considered as offsets to total costs. The choice of whether associated revenues should be treated as a cost offset or a side benefit should not significantly affect the program decision, since in either case the revenues will have been explicity considered.

Summary tables in the program analysis report should probably display three lines for each program alternative: total costs, offsetting revenues, and the net cost to the government.

7. *Some alternatives may affect the costs of other program areas.* A slum clearance program might result in future reductions in the need for fire and crime protection services for the cleared area; on the other hand, it might

also lead to increased demand for park and recreation services.[3] These can be important considerations, especially for analyses considering large-scale changes. Estimating such effects is often complex and particularly difficult.

8. *If resources are put into one program, opportunities to use the same resources elsewhere have been foregone.* The value of these foregone opportunities is the "opportunity cost" of putting resources into the selected program. This "value" is, therefore, relevant to program selection.

In program analysis, the explicit identification and assessment of alternatives is a practical way to take account of opportunity costs. To illustrate, a government might use land it already owns for a new public facility. It would not incur any additional land costs, but would be giving up the opportunity to use the land for other purposes. The alternative use of the land is an important consideration. The analysis might attempt to impute a dollar value to this land (perhaps using current market value) and include this imputed value as a cost. Or it might avoid this imputation and instead consider other land uses as explicit alternatives to be evaluated. *If imputed values are used, since they are not actual dollar outlays, they should be separately identified so as not to distort the estimation of funding outlays actually needed for an alternative.* However, if one option was, for example, to sell government land, then the resulting revenues (perhaps including any taxes generated by the land or improvements to it) would be an important alternative opportunity.

Where land or facilities have other meaningful uses, the analysis should at least explicitly indicate as a "negative benefit" or undesirable effect the loss of the land for these other future uses.

Estimating Costs

Six approaches or sources for estimating costs follow:

1. Current data applied to the future;
2. "Vendor" estimates;
3. Internal "engineering" estimates;

---

3. Some financial repercussions of a program might also occur *outside* the government. For example, changes to transportation systems or in housing may have considerable effects on many types of businesses in the area—some favorable, some unfavorable. Or the gain in future earnings to individual citizens due to improved education or employment programs also may mean increased tax revenue. However, those outside-the-government cost effects should be distinguished from the inside-the-government costs and probably are better considered as economic impacts to be included in effectiveness estimation than as part of the cost analysis.

4. Costs from other jurisdictions;
5. Statistical estimation; and
6. Cost factors and cost models.

For any given analysis some or all of these approaches might be used. Each of these is discussed briefly:

1. *Current data applied to the future*. This costing approach is primarily applicable to costs that are not expected to change significantly. As an example, the latest salary and employee benefit scales might simply be used to estimate future personnel costs. Current data on the number of personnel or staff-hours required to perform a specific task might be used to estimate the future requirements for that task, if the task appears stable.

There are severe limitations to this approach, particularly if demand for a service changes or if technological improvements in equipment are anticipated. If, for example, a government's emergency rescue vehicles are expected to become more complex in the future (e.g., more automatic monitoring or telecommunications devices and emergency equipment), higher costs per vehicle might be anticipated. There also might be higher maintenance costs and additional training costs for operation. In this case, it would not be appropriate to use unadjusted current data.

Price level changes may, of course, also affect the future costs of program components even if nothing else changes. This problem is discussed later.

2. *"Vendor" estimates*. Some programs involve pieces of equipment or facilities for which price quotations can be obtained from a seller or builder. If quotes are for existing items or items with minor modifications, prices should be accurate. However, a firm commitment is not always implied in the estimate, and complications might arise in obtaining the item in the future at the estimated price.

3. *Internal "engineering" estimates*. As new programs are proposed that involve components significantly different from current or past program components, other techniques are needed. The major technique currently in use is to employ technical experts—government employees or consultants—to prepare cost estimates for the new components. For example, city or state engineers or others doing program design may also estimate costs.

One problem with engineering estimates is that a lot of time may be required if many program alternatives and variations are to be examined.

4. *Costs from other jurisdictions*. Sometimes analysts can use cost information provided by other governments. This can be useful when other

governments have had experience with a particular program alternative for which the jurisdiction doing the analysis has had little or no experience. The cost information can be obtained by combinations of mail, telephone, and on-site data collection. The analysts must be very careful to learn what the costs from the other governments cover and do not cover—and under what conditions the program operated. Only then can the analysts determine to what extent the costs are applicable to their own jurisdiction and are comparable with costs obtained for other program alternatives.

For example, the Delaware Department of Corrections did an analysis comparing inmate food services under contract versus food services managed by state employees at its correctional facilities. The analysis team obtained cost information from seven other state departments of corrections that had recently contracted for inmate food service. A key issue in the comparability of the cost numbers became whether or not the contracted prices included kitchen security and food warehousing, and the extent to which food was procured (and paid for) by the contractor rather than the state agency. The analysts found that some of the costs figures from the other states were reasonably comparable and could be used, but others could not.[4]

5. *Statistical estimation.* This method is less commonly used in most state and local governments.

Predicting future costs, especially for programs with new and perhaps unusual characteristics, is a very difficult task. Expert judgment will be helpful and necessary, but cost analysis may be aided considerably by the use of statistical techniques. Statistics on past performance may permit inferences about future costs or performance.

The use of statistics can be very simple or very complicated. The simpler techniques of statistics are familiar. For example, to derive a figure for the fuel and maintenance cost of police cars used in a traffic control program, the previous year's costs for all traffic control police cars can be divided by the number of cars to obtain an average cost per car. Assuming no price increases or significant changes in the nature of the police cars to be used, the average cost per car could then be used to estimate the cost of proposed alternative programs involving any number of police cars of the same type.

A more advanced technique is *regression analysis*. In the example shown in exhibit 19, the analysts used a "simple" regression analysis to estimate the future maintenance costs of government vehicles. The analysts assumed that the major explanatory variable in the cost equation was the number of

---

4. Delaware, State of, "Report on Service Alternatives for Food Services," Smyrna, Delaware: State of Delaware Department of Corrections, July 16, 1987.

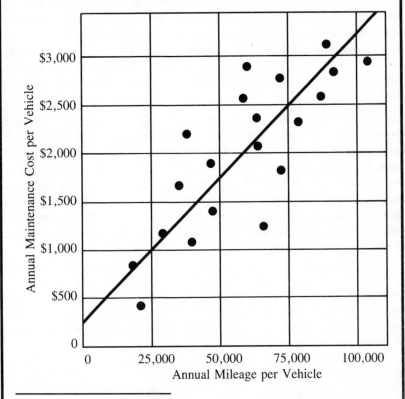

Exhibit 19.   AN EXAMPLE OF REGRESSION ANALYSIS:
ESTIMATED ANNUAL MAINTENANCE COSTS
PER VEHICLE

Estimated Cost = $250 + $.03 × miles driven
(If a vehicle were to be driven 75,000 miles next
year, the estimated maintenance costs would be
$2,500.)

Source: The George Washington University State-Local Finances Project, "The
Role and Nature of Cost Analysis in a PPB System" (Washington, D.C., June 1968).
● = Actual costs and miles driven by an individual vehicle in the last year.

miles driven. The diagram shows a hypothetical "scatter diagram" on which are plotted the most recent year's data on the existing vehicles. From the appearance of the scatter diagram, the analysts estimate that a sraight line would fit the data. Using standard mathematical procedures (with some computer assistance) a line of "best fit" can be derived and is shown on the scatter diagram. The equation for the line is also shown. The resulting equation can then be used to help estimate future maintenance costs of vehicles of a type similar to those in the sample.

In many analyses, considerably more complicated assumptions may be necessary, requiring more complex statistical techniques and more complex equations. With more than one explanatory variable, "multiple" regression analysis rather than "simple" regression analysis is required.

To use such equations for estimating future program costs, it is first necessary to estimate the future values for each of the explanatory variables, that is, the "annual mileage per vehicle" in exhibit 19. This itself may often be difficult.

6. *Cost factors and cost models.* There may be a need in a particular program analysis for the examination of numerous program alternatives. For some government services, fairly frequent program analyses may be needed. Thus, there may develop a repetitive need for the preparation of cost factors and cost equations that can be applied to many different costing problems. Statistical equations such as those already illustrated as well as simple cost factors—such as the annual maintenance cost per unit—might be appropriate for each major program area. These would be updated periodically for use as costing problems arose.

Individual cost factors or cost equations might be prepared at any convenient level of aggregation. For example, some might cover a single accounting object class, others might cover a subdivision of an object class, and still others an aggregation of object classes. This will depend upon the particular circumstances such as the nature of the available data and the use to which the factors and equations will be put.

These cost factors and cost equations together could provide estimates of the total program cost for different variations of a certain type of program. This can be called a "cost model." Such cost models might be constructed for different types of programs. If the cost model involves much computation and is used frequently enough, computerization is likely to be appropriate.

Some Special Problems in Cost Analysis

Four special problems need to be mentioned:

1. First is the issue of price changes. Should adjustments be made to reflect possible future price changes in the various elements of cost? This

problem is particularly important if some of the alternatives are likely to be more affected by future price increases than others. Estimating future changes in general price levels is difficult. In addition to the problem of attempting to predict the trend of the economy, the price index is likely to differ for each element of cost. That is, the cost of payroll, of construction, and of various types of equipment each potentially requires its own price index. One concern is that the price level estimates could be self-fulfilling—that contractors, unions, or other claimant groups would become aware of the estimates and would be unlikely to settle for less than the estimated increases.

Perhaps such projections should be made only when it appears clear that the program choice could be significantly affected by price changes.

2. A second special problem in program cost analysis is the need to provide some indication of the magnitude of uncertainty of the cost estimates. Estimates of costs and effectiveness will seldom be precise, especially for years beyond the next budget year. Estimates to within 10 to 25 percent for unfamiliar alternatives will often be as accurate as can be expected. The magnitude and likelihood of cost uncertainties may affect final program decisions and should, if significant, be assessed as well as possible. Techniques may range from simply labeling estimates as "reasonably accurate" or "highly uncertain" to more elaborate techniques which attempt to estimate quantitatively the likelihood and size of the uncertainty. Handling uncertainty is discussed further in chapter 7.

3. A third special problem in cost analysis is how to summarize future costs for each program alternative. Four options are:

a. Present the cost for each year;
b. Describe in the aggregate all costs for a given number of years;
c. Calculate the "present worth" or "present value" of the expected outlays; and
d. A combination of the above.

The "present-worth" technique requires the government to select a specific rate of return (i.e., an "interest" or "discount" rate). Then analysts compute the present worth of the expenditures for each future year for each program alternative. For example, an alternative might require the expenditure of $1 million now, $1 million a year from now, and $1 million two years from now. Assuming an annual discount rate of 10 percent, approximately $2.74 million invested today at 10 percent interest would provide just enough to meet the three $1 million payments. Other expenditure patterns could similarly be translated into present worths. A second program requiring expenditures of $0.2 million now and $1.4 million in each of the next two years is equivalent to about $2.63 million now invested at a rate of 10 percent. Therefore, other things being equal, the second program is more desirable because its present worth is less, even though both programs require the same outlays of funds.

A major problem in using the present-worth technique is the selection of the appropriate interest rate. This selection is difficult and controversial.

In most individual program analyses, the consideration of the present worth of future flow of costs will not alter the choice of programs and therefore may not be worth the effort. The present-worth technique should be used primarily when alternatives with similar total costs but considerably different time phasing of expenditures are under examination.

4. Finally, there is a tendency in cost analysis to attempt to be overly precise in situations that do not warrant it. This can be both wasteful of effort and misleading. The amount of precision, possible and needed, decreases to the extent that estimates are made for years beyond the immediate year for program alternatives that require departures from current methods. Analysts should explicitly estimate how much precision is needed, then should adjust cost analysis accordingly.

Chapter 5
Estimating Effectiveness

It is difficult to estimate how effective an existing program will be in the future. It is even more challenging to predict the consequences of new or modified programs. But estimates, even crude, are necessary.

The basic problems are the future uncertainties about conditions under which a proposed program will have to operate and the likelihood of success under those conditions. The further one projects a program into the future, the more uncertain one's projections become; even a one-year projection can entail considerable uncertainty.

The more that is known about a program alternative and the conditions in which it will operate, the easier and more accurate the projection will be. Inevitably, estimating the effectiveness of a program requires many assumptions about the relation between government resources (including the ways these resources are combined and put to use) and outcomes. This is a large part of the art and craft of program analysis.

It is difficult to describe the many approaches that can be used to estimate future program effectiveness and the innumerable situations and variations program analyts can expect to face. However, an attempt is necessary. Nine general approaches are identified below. These approaches are somewhat similar to those described for estimating program costs. We distinguish between approaches for estimating the effectiveness of those programs that are extensions or minor variations of a government's existing programs, and those used for programs that are new. The approaches are summarized in exhibit 20.[1]

---

1. An approach to estimating effectiveness that is often used—but which we feel is rarely appropriate—is to assume that effectiveness is proportional to the amount of inputs, or resources, applied. One can, for example, assume that adding 10 percent to the amount of resources applied to a service will improve the quality of the service by 10 percent. This approach has the advantage of simplicity, but, of course, it begs the question of whether more resources will help and, for given combinations of resources, how much is needed.

Exhibit 20.   APPROACHES TO ESTIMATING
                EFFECTIVENESS

Approaches for Extensions or Minor Variations of Existing Programs

1. Use past performance as the estimate of future effectiveness.
2. Adjust past performance by estimates of future conditions affecting effectiveness.

Approaches for Alternatives New to the Jurisdiction

3. Use past performance in other governments as the estimate for future effectiveness.
4. Obtain performance estimates from vendor.
5. Develop "engineered" estimates.
6. Employ mathematical modeling techniques.
7. Use "expert" judgment.
8. Use a "simulated adversary" process.
9. Use information from a limited trial of the program.

Estimating Effectiveness for Alternatives that Are Extensions or Minor Variations of Existing Programs

1. *Data on the performance of past programs might be used in estimates of future performance.* Unfortunately, information on existing programs is often scarce and a special program evaluation is likely to be required.[2] In addition, the use of past performance information assumes that conditions will not change substantially in the future. For example, if the criminal apprehension rate for the past year is 20 percent, this figure might be used as an estimate of continuing the same program into the future. This approach is certainly simple, but it is probably overused. The assumption of performance stability is questionable in many, if not most, cases.

---

2. A discussion of the procedures of program evaluation oriented toward state and local government personnel is presented in Harry Hatry et al., *Practical Program Evaluation for State and Local Governments* (Washington, D.C.: The Urban Institute, 1981). Other, more detailed works on program evaluation include Cook and Campbell (1979); Fitz-Gibbon and Morris (1978); Reichen and Boruch (1974); Rossi and Freeman (1982); Suchman (1967); and Weiss (1972).

2. *Past performance data can be adjusted by estimating likely effects of changes in future conditions on performance.* There are many ways to do this. One entails the use of time series data. Rather than using only performance data for the past year, an analyst takes an average of several past years' performance data or uses the data of several years to compute a projection line based on recent trends. For example, if the crime apprehension rate for the past year is 20 percent, and if in prior years the rate had been gradually increasing, a higher apprehension rate would be used in projections. The assumption is that the trend over a number of years is a more reliable indicator of the future than a single year's data.

Time alone should not be considered an adequate explanation of future conditions in most situations. Changes in the overall population, in client mix (such as age, sex, income, race, and residential location), and in physical characteristics of the jurisdiction (such as new housing and transportation) may affect the performance of program alternatives. While the effects can become quite complex, the analyst can often identify certain key conditions that are changing. Once these changes are identified, their effects can be projected into the future and used to modify estimates of the program's effectiveness. For example, an examination of solid waste landfill disposal alternatives would require, in part, projections of changes in the numbers of households and of waste generated per household. This would yield an estimate of future demand for solid waste disposal by residential units; this estimate could then be added to estimates of waste from other sources and be compared with present disposal capacity and the capacity of other landfill options to determine how effective each is in handling projected future needs.

Estimating Effectiveness for Alternatives that Are New to the Government

3. *If a proposed alternative has been tried by other governments, useful data from those government experiences may be available.* These data, however, may not be fully relevant because governments seldom routinely collect evaluative information, and conditions in the other governments may be quite different. Analysts should be cautious when using published reports, since they may be mainly public relations documents and may not have been based on systematic program evaluation.

Analysts may need to make onsite visits to obtain detailed program descriptions and performance data. This was a key step, for example, in the Fort Worth program analysis of the Indianapolis police take-home car plan.[3]

---

3. See Donald Fisk, *The Indianapolis Police Fleet Plan* (Washington, D.C.: The Urban Institute, 1970).

Consideration of the plan in Fort Worth was prompted by reports of its use by the Indianapolis Police Department. Fort Worth personnel, with the help of a consultant, undertook a systematic evaluation of the costs and effects of the program experience to date in Indianapolis, with the cooperation of that city. That information was used in estimating costs and effects of a similar plan for Fort Worth.

Another example is the use of a new sewer repair (relining) procedure called Instituform, rather than pipe replacement. This was initially tried in Maryland counties based on performance information from other cities.[4] Information was obtained on the procedure's ability to reduce traffic disruption and on the durability of the process.

Another example is analyses by the State of Delaware Departments of Correction and Administrative Services, respectively, of the possibility of contracting inmate food service and fleet vehicle maintenance. These departments surveyed by mail and telephone other states that had contracted— in order to obtain information on service quality and cost for use in comparing contracting to Delaware's current service approach. (Chapter 8 discusses these two examples further.)

Performance reports prepared shortly after the initiation of a program should be considered with caution. A program may take six to twelve months, and often longer, before its operation stabilizes.

Even if good evaluative information from other jurisdictions is available, the need for an independent analysis of the program remains. The attractiveness of any alternative depends in part on conditions in a particular state or local jurisdiction. For example, before making a decision on a police take-home car plan, a city should consider how many of its reported crimes could be prevented by use of marked police cars.

4. *In some circumstances, vendors can provide performance estimates for equipment-oriented alternatives, or at least performance information on the equipment itself.* Vendor estimates, of course, can be expected to be optimistic; they are also likely to be limited to the immediate intended performance of the equipment and not to the variety of impacts—especially negative ones—that may occur when the equipment is used by human beings in less than ideal working environments.

5. *In some cases, the analyst has to synthesize an estimate from known facts about the alternative, or even use "engineered" estimates based on anticipated characteristics of the proposed system.* This is particularly so with

---

4. Hatry and Steinthal (1984), p. 66.

alternatives that involve new technologies or new procedures for which appropriate comparison data are not available. For example, a new solid waste disposal system might be crudely assessed by using data from the design and technical specifications to estimate the amount of waste that the system could handle on a daily basis and the amount of pollution that it would yield.

Analysts should also assess whether the estimated effectiveness is likely to remain the same or change significantly in the years following introduction. If significant changes seem likely, crude estimates of the amount of the change should be made. This type of analysis is filled with uncertainties, however, and new technologies rarely perform, at least at first, as well as anticipated.

6. *At times, various mathematical modeling techniques can be used.* Formal models are particularly useful where (a) there are many and complex interactions among the factors affecting program effectiveness, and (b) historical performance data are available and can be used in quantitative form.[5]

Analyses of the number and location of emergency ambulances and fire stations have used models to make response time calculations. In these cases a major element in effectiveness calculations is the attempt to estimate travel time from a fire station or ambulance location to the fire or client needing emergency care. Mathematical models are used to simulate the geographical network in a jurisdiction. Analysts can compute response times for varying numbers and locations of fire stations or ambulances, so as to select the configuration that minimizes response time. Considerable data on the existing street network and vehicle speeds are required by the models. It would be desirable to consider likely future changes in the street network and vehicles in order to make the network and vehicle speeds more appropriate to expected future conditions.[6]

A variety of mathematical modeling techniques, some requiring computer assistance, have been used to allocate police resources by time of day and day of week, to route garbage trucks, and to select toll booth arrangements. However, analysts can often use less complex and non-computer-based mathematical models. Separate analyses by two cities to allocate fireboats in order to protect the waterfront involved fairly simple mappings of the placement

---

5. A survey of federally supported models, including a listing by subject area, is contained in Gary Fromm, William L. Hamilton and Diane E. Hamilton, *Federally Supported Mathematical Models*, NTIS-PB 241562 (Washington, D.C.: Data Resources, Inc. and ABT Associates, Inc., June 1974). The survey also provides model cost information.

6. For further discussions see: Kenneth L. Kraemer, *A Systems Approach to Decision Making—Policy Analyses in Local Government* (Washington, D.C.: The International City Management Association, 1973); and Thomas R. Willemain, "The Status of Performance Measures for Emergency Medical Services" (Cambridge, Massachusetts: Operations Research Center, Massachusetts Institute of Technology, July 1974).

of fireboats relative to projected call locations and frequency. If the number of combinations examined had been greater, a computerized approach might have been more efficient.

Mathematical modeling might be used to directly estimate a service's effectiveness or to project intermediate factors affecting future demand for a service so that alternatives could be rated against them. A variety of statistical, operations research, and mathematical techniques are available that on occasion will be quite useful.

A word of caution on the use of models is necessary.[7] The critical assumptions built into models must be clearly articulated by the model builders and understood by the decision makers, since these assumptions usually influence the results significantly. Too often large models become so complex that only the computer knows what is going on. Model applications need to be reviewed beforehand to determine the probable amount of improvement over simpler approaches. Large-scale models requiring computer processing are expensive to develop and to "debug" for proper operation. The greatest payoffs from a large model are likely to occur where they are used often enough—or on extremely important and costly program decisions—to justify the initial development and programming costs.

7. *To supplement previous methods, expert judgment may be appropriate.* Experts may be government personnel or persons outside who have extensive experience in the program area. Their judgments can be employed in making direct estimates of an alternative's effectiveness or for estimating the future values of factors needed for effectiveness calculations. A systematic procedure for making judgments should be used, and the judgments should be documented and substantiated as well as possible. Approaches such as Delphi, which use anonymous opinions of a number of experts to refine progressively a specific projection, can sometimes be helpful.[8] But these sophisticated approaches tend to be time-consuming and relatively expensive; they are probably justifiable only if other satisfactory approaches are not available.

In the Nashville analysis of its system for the short-term care of neglected-dependent children (described in appendix A-1), the analysts used social

---

7. Two criticisms of large-scale model efforts are contained in Douglas B. Lee, Jr., "Requiem for Large-Scale Models," *Journal of the American Institute of Planners*, May 1973; and Ida R. Hoos, *Systems Analysis in Public Policy—A Critique* (Berkeley, California: University of California Press, 1972).

8. See, for example, H. Sackman, *Delphi Assessment: Expert Opinion, Forecasting, and Group Process*, RAND Publication R-1238-PR (Santa Monica, California: The Rand Corporation, April 1974).

workers to examine case records from the previous year. The social workers were asked to estimate, for each case, the likely effectiveness in avoiding short-term placement in the county children's home if early screening had been done.

Experts could be used merely to *rank* the relative effectiveness of alternatives in terms of a particular characteristic, but quantitative *ratings* of effectiveness are preferable. For example, analysts might want to assess the degree to which various probation and parole service approaches would lead to a reduction in recidivism. At the very least, a number of experts might rank each proposed approach as "better," "worse," or "about the same" as the existing approach. More useful for the purposes of analysis (but more difficult for the expert) would be estimates of the degree of likely success of alternatives.

8. *A "simulated adversary process" may sometimes be appropriate.* Under this approach, each major alternative is assigned to a different "team." Each team then builds as strong a case as possible for its assigned alternative, probably using some of the techniques already described. This approach is appropriate primarily when analysts are dealing with important issues that will have differing impacts on groups in the community. In such cases the approach may provide government officials with a broadened perspective on the pros and cons of the various alternatives.

9. *Finally, the government might undertake a limited trial of a new program if sound estimates are not obtainable, and if government officials believe that a particular alternative has considerable potential but that uncertainties are too great for a full-scale commitment.* This approach is appropriate in cases where a short-term program of limited scope is feasible and where only small initial investments are needed for personnel and capital additions. The trial approach has another advantage when past experience is not available: a trial is likely to detect unintended, perhaps negative, program effects.

One example of the trial approach is in crime control where it is extremely difficult to predict the effectiveness of various manpower allocation or patrol strategies such as team policing. In such cases the government might undertake a one-year trial of a specific strategy in particular neighborhoods to obtain information on effectiveness.

Many difficulties are associated with this approach. For example, some programs may not be adequately evaluated on the basis of a one-year experience. Start-up problems might temporarily degrade performance and produce inaccurate indications of long-term performance. On the other hand, special attention paid to a program might result in better short-term performance and yield misleading indications of long-term performance.

Trials are often conducted without adequate concern for performance data. As a result, the government is likely to have very little information about program effectiveness by the end of the trial period.[9] If a government uses the trial approach, it should provide for a systematic program evaluation.[10] The trial should be designed realistically, and critical evaluation criteria should be identified in advance.

Illustrations of Some Approaches

Due to the numerous variations in program alternatives and to the problems of effectiveness estimation, generalizations about appropriate effectiveness estimation procedures are difficult to make. In most instances, a combination of the techniques enumerated above will be appropriate. The following examples—and the more detailed presentations in chapter 8 and appendix A—illustrate typical problems and the ways that specific techniques might be applied.

1. Neglected and Dependent Children

In an analysis of ways to reduce the number of neglected and dependent children and particularly the number placed in a children's institution (described in more detail in appendix A-1), estimates were sought of the effectiveness of increasing emergency homemaker service, increasing emergency foster homes, and providing initial screening of requests for neglected and dependent care. Each of the previous year's cases in which a child received neglected and dependent services was categorized as to the reason for the child coming into the system. A professional social worker examined these cases and made judgments as to when an emergency homemaker, an emergency foster home, or initial screening could have been used to keep children in their own home or in the home of someone who could provide appropriate

---

9. Note that, as discussed in chapter 3 in the section on the search for alternatives, the option of undertaking a limited trial of a new program is itself an alternative that needs to be assessed as to its costs and effects—and compared with those of going ahead with one of the alternatives without such a trial.

10. A detailed discussion of program evaluation is contained in a companion volume, Harry Hatry et al., *Practical Program Evaluation for State and Local Governments* (Washington, D.C.: The Urban Institute, 1981).

care. The number and percent of cases in which a child could have avoided being institutionalized were then calculated.

The number of children entering the child care system and their reasons for entering were assumed to be the same in future years as in the most recent year for which data were available. If more time had been allowed, the analysts might have collected data from past years for a time trend analysis to project more accurately the number of children of the various types likely to enter the system in future years. Professional judgment could then have been used to estimate the number of children of each type who could avoid institutionalization through the additional services provided by each proposed option. A more extensive analysis might have examined the changing population makeup in the county (using statistical analysis) to project any significant changes in population characteristics and the likely effects of these population changes on the type and number of neglected-dependent children in the future (considering such factors as increasing or decreasing affluence in the county among parents with children under 18 years old.)

2. Ambulances, Fire Stations, and Patrol Cars

Analyses of the desired number and location of emergency ambulances, fire stations, or police patrol cars have generally used response time as the measure of effectiveness. This measure however, does not take into account the value of reduced response time in saving lives, reducing fire damage, or apprehending criminals. This makes it difficult to determine whether the expense of added stations, ambulances, or patrol cars and the accompanying reduction in response time is worth the additional cost. Without such information, decisions may be based on relatively uninformed judgments.

To improve the information available for such decisions, experts might be used to estimate the impacts of various response time rates for particular client conditions. By examining past ambulance cases, analysts and medical experts could identify a series of representative scenarios. They might, for example, specify the type of problems leading to the call for an ambulance, the patient's condition at the time of the call, and such critical patient characteristics as age. The medical experts would then estimate the likely effects of various delay times. In a more ambitious analysis, the effects of various delay times might be estimated more reliably by examining a large number of actual cases on which response time, patient data, and patient outcome information were available. Statistical analysis would then be used to help estimate the effects of various response times. The analysts and experts could estimate the probable frequency of each scenario from examining the frequency of past cases.

A time series analysis could be used to adjust past frequencies and project trends in the number of each type of case. The analysts would then be able to estimate the number of patients who would be helped by various reductions in response time as a result of changes in the number and stationing of ambulances.

3. Helicopters

To analyze the potential value of helicopters in apprehending crime suspects, a sample of past crime incidences might be examined to determine whether a helicopter might have been useful in each situation. Such conditions as weather, visibility, location, and circumstances of the crime would be included in the consideration. Expert judgment—perhaps by police officers from cities that use helicopters—would be used to estimate the potential consequences of the use of the helicopters in each instance. The frequency of cases in which helicopters would be helpful would be calculated from the statistical sample of incidents (after adjusting for possible factors that would affect the future frequency of each type of circumstance).

4. Parole and Probation Counselors

A difficult type of analysis problem—a kind that frequently arises in social service programs—occurs in considering whether to increase the number of parole and probation counselors. Of particular concern is the effect, if any, of changes in the caseload per worker on client recidivism. The analysis might begin by making estimates of future caseloads (categorized by the type of offender), based on past caseload trends and recent policies of the courts and law enforcement agencies.

The analysis might then examine the past effectiveness of the current parole and probation officer staff in terms of both (1) the number and percent of cases in which probation or parole revocations occurred, and (2) the number and percent with criminal records *after* completing probation-parole (perhaps determined by follow-ups on a sample of former parolees or probationers).

Three approaches might be used to estimate the amount of improvement from reduced caseloads: (a) Undertake a carefully monitored trial to determine the effects of caseload reduction. Preferably this would include "control" and "experimental" groups created by randomly assigning probationers and parolees to counselors with varying caseloads. This approach would require many months before adequate impact data became available. (b) Examine a sample of past cases to identify, by category of parolee, the amount of counseling provided and the apparent success for various levels of effort. (c) Have professionals examine past cases to estimate the degree to which the individual might have been helped if various amounts of additional time had been provided (a ''scenario'' approach).

5. Drug Abuse Treatment

In a drug abuse treatment program (and, in fact, for most rehabilitation programs), it is important to classify clients in terms of the expected difficulty of rehabilitation. Programs that treat clients with severe drug problems and low levels of motivation probably have lower rehabilitation rates than programs that treat clients with less severe drug problems and higher levels of motivation. Expected rehabilitation rates should be estimated for each level of client difficulty. Estimates of the likely number of persons in each category in the future are required to estimate the number of persons likely to be rehabilitated by each alternative treatment program. Rehabilitation rates for the various client categories might be calculated by using past rehabilitation rates from existing programs or similar programs of other governments or by using expert judgment. Appendix A-3 describes in more detail the estimating effectiveness of drug treatment programs.

6. Welfare Staffs

Suppose a state or county public welfare agency wants to assess a proposal to increase its quality control staff that check the accuracy of welfare eligibility determinations, payment amounts, and other payment errors. Analysts could review existing inspection results or make a special investigation of a random sample of cases to determine the percentage of investigated cases with inaccurate payments and the average dollar amount involved in each error. This percentage might be assumed to apply also to the future. It would then be necessary to estimate how many inequities would be uncovered by additional case inspections. For example, if the sampling of cases indicated inaccuracies in one out of ten cases, then about ten investigations would be required per error found. (This ratio could be reduced if the analysts examined cases to identify those types of cases that seemed to be most associated with errors. The agency's quality-control staff could then focus on these cases. The program analysts would need to estimate the time required to identify such error-prone cases and the rate of errors found.) Estimates of the amount of time required per inspector could be based on past experience with various types of cases. The number and amount of incorrect payments and the resulting corrections (and overall savings) could then be estimated for the number of investigators proposed.

7. Solid Waste Disposal

An analysis of future solid waste disposal alternatives might contain the following steps:

(a) Projections of solid waste generated in the future would be based on projections of the population, the amount of waste generated per capita (which itself might be changing), and any projected changes in industries. These projections of future need might be made by statistical means including time trend projection as well as by more complicated approaches that utilize a number of variables in addition to time.

(b) Estimates of the treatment capacity (for each type of refuse) of each solid waste disposal alternative would be based on the technical characteristics of each option. "Engineering" calculations might be needed for new technological alternatives.

(c) The capabilities estimated in (b) could then be compared with the need estimated in (a) to indicate the capacity of each alternative to meet the need. Because of the long lead time before certain alternatives become operational (for example, when an alternative requires the construction of new facilities) and because of the likely annual growth of solid waste, the ability of each alternative to dispose of waste probably should be considered for each future year relevant to the analysis.

(d) Estimates of the remaining pollution generated by each alternative would be based on the amount of waste disposed and the technical characteristics of each disposal alternative, estimated by "engineering" calculations. It would be desirable to estimate the resulting ambient quality of the air or water and resulting hazard levels. This would involve difficult steps, considering such factors as the likely future of air or water quality from all other sources, weather conditions, and the interaction of various pollutants.

Final Comment on Effectiveness Measurement

These examples merely scratch the surface by illustrating the great variety of effectiveness estimation issues that are likely to arise even in a single state or local government. The examples do not include detailed how-to-do-it suggestions. But they may suggest ideas as to starting points for estimating effectiveness in individual analyses.

Chapter 6
Implementation Feasibility ("IF") Analysis

Government policymakers inevitably consider feasibility of implementation (explicitly or implicitly) as a central criterion in making their decisions. In sharp contrast, program analysts seldom assess the feasibility of putting alternatives into operation. Analysts usually assume that each alternative would be equally easy to set up and operate in the approximate form developed in the analysis. But implementation problems may increase the cost of an alternative, decrease its effectiveness, create delay, and even prevent it from being used.

As discussed later in chapter 8, governments in recent years have been giving more consideration to more radical service delivery options, sometimes referred to as "privatization." These options include the expansion of the use of contracting, greater use of volunteers, providing vouchers to clients, and a variety of public-private partnerships. Options such as these raise major feasibility issues, issues that can have a great effect on final program decisions.

A systematic, explicit treatment of feasibility would:

1. Identify possible impacts of implementation on cost and program effectiveness, including timing, so that estimates are more realistic;

2. Provide a comparison of the feasibility of implementing different alternatives to alert public officials to special efforts needed to implement them; and

3. Suggest means by which implementation might be eased by revising alternatives.

Since program analyses have seldom explicitly examined implementation feasibility, any attempt to outline systematic procedures for doing so has little precedent. There are, however, a few case studies that can be called upon.[1] Though it is beyond the scope of this work to give a full treatment to this subject, some initial suggestions can be presented. Exhibit 21 contains a checklist of factors affecting feasibility of an alternative. Appendix D provides another example of such a list, one tailored specifically for use when considering alternative service delivery approaches such as contracting out an activity.

What Might Analysts Do Regarding Implementation Feasibility?

There are a number of different roles for the analyst in Implementation Feasibility ("IF") analysis:

1. *At a minimum, analysts should attempt to indicate the overall potential impacts of difficulties in implementation on the costs and effectiveness of each alternative.* Possible delays in implementation should be identified. Analysts and proponents of alternatives often minimize the amount of lead time required for approval and implementation. Findings of an analysis are usually not sensitive to delays in implementation of a few months. Implementation, however, can be delayed for many months, or even years. Expected delays should be identified explicitly and considered in estimates of costs and effectiveness.

2. *The analysts might identify and attempt to quantify the main implementation difficulties of each alternative.* The checklist in exhibit 21 can be used as a starting point. This information can serve as an additional criterion for making program choices. Two approaches might be used:

Alternatives might be ranked. For example, "Alternative A is likely to be more difficult to implement than Alternatives B and C," "Alternative C is more difficult than D," etc.

Alternatives might be rated, perhaps using "expert" judgment or some arbitrary scale to yield an implementation feasibility score. For example,

---

1. See, for example: Martha A. Derthick, *New Towns In-Town: Why a Federal Program Failed* (Washington, D.C.: The Urban Institute, 1972); Jeffrey L. Pressman and Aaron B. Wildavsky, *Implementation* (Berkeley: University of California Press, 1973); Erwin C. Hargrove, "The Missing Link: The Study of Implementation," Working Paper (Washington, D.C.: The Urban Institute, July 1975); The Urban Institute and Council of State Governments, "Alternatives Analysis: A Process for Periodic Reviews of Alternative Ways To Deliver State Services," Working Paper (Washington, D.C.: The Urban Institute, 1987).

In addition to the case studies, see Anthony Downs, *Inside Bureaucracy*, Rand Corporation Research Study (Boston: Little Brown and Co., 1967), for a discussion of the closely related issue of "bureaucratic behavior."

Exhibit 21. FACTORS TO EXAMINE IN ASSESSING
IMPLEMENTATION FEASIBILITY OF EACH
PROGRAM ALTERNATIVE

1. *How many agencies [both internal and external to the government] must cooperate or participate in order to ensure successful implementation?* In some cases, agencies of other governments or organizations in the private sector (such as businesses or citizen groups) might be involved. Since these groups are not responsible to a governmental unit, their actions may render any given alternative infeasible. The more people and groups that must provide approval or support, the more difficult implementation is likely to be. External agencies might be weighted more than internal agencies in estimating implementation difficulty.

2. *To what extent does the alternative directly affect services in a way clearly visible to the public? Are there existing client groups whose interests will be affected, particularly by a change in existing services?* Alternatives that propose maintaining or increasing existing levels of services will be less likely to present implementation difficulties than ones that reduce the level of service. For example, the choice of different types of refuse collection vehicles will be less controversial than the question of whether refuse should be collected at the curb instead of at the back door.

3. *To what extent does the alternative threaten important officials with reductions in power, prestige, or privilege?* These individuals can be expected to resist implementation.

4. *To what extent does the alternative threaten jobs?* Where a strong employees' organization is present, opposition can be great. Special compensation might be required to gain acceptance. Cost savings may be considerably less than initially estimated.

5. *To what extent are special personnel capabilities required?* Will additional training be required? Are there required personnel within the civil service system? If not, can provision be made for obtaining them?

6. *To what extent does the alternative require changes in the behavior of governmental employees?* Employees may be unable or unwilling to behave as

Exhibit 21 (continued)

required. For example, an alternative may involve assumptions about police officer behavior toward suspected criminals or the care with which solid waste collectors handle containers. Or it may require a change in working hours or location of employees that might lead to resistance.

7. *Are sources and availability of funds fairly definite? To what extent does the alternative call for added funds in the face of tight revenue constraints?* Some sources of funds may be more available than others. Alternatives that involve special funding support may be subject to considerable uncertainties. An alternative that requires bond issue approval is likely to encounter both uncertainty and delays.

8. *Are complicated legal questions involved? Are changes such as new legislation required? What is the likelihood that these changes would be made?* At the very least, this factor, if present, will probably impose delays.

9. *To what extent has public debate galvanized opinions for or against the alternative?*

10. *To what extent does the alternative require space or facilities that may be difficult to obtain?* For example, neighborhood populations may resist locating drug treatment centers, mental health facilities, nursing homes, half-way homes, etc., in their neighborhoods.

11. *To what extent does the alternative involve significant technological uncertainties?* New technologies typically involve operational problems that may increase costs, reduce effectiveness, and delay or even prevent implementation.

12. *Has a recent crisis lent support to one of the alternatives?* Implementation difficulties might be alleviated if the problem is clearly recognized by the community. For example, a wave of burglaries might greatly improve chances of gaining rapid acceptance for more police patrol units. On the other hand, programs that emphasize prevention before a problem is generally recognized tend to be more difficult to sell. (Note that one of the advantages of systematic analysis is the opportunity to identify emerging problems and to produce evidence for encouraging preventive action.)

Alternative A may be rated as "very difficult" or given a numerical rating of 10 on a scale of 1 to 10 in order of increasing difficulty. Alternative B might be rated as "difficult" and given a rating of 7. Alternative C might be rated as the "least difficult to implement" and given a rating of 3.

In both approaches each implementation factor, such as those in exhibit 21, could be rated or ranked. Exhibit 22 displays a chart and rating scale that a number of State of Delaware and State of Maryland operating departments used in 1987 in their assessments of the feasibility of various options for greater use of the private sector in service delivery (such as contracting with private firms).

Ratings do present difficulties. However, if procedures are understandable and clear to users, and if component ratings for each factor as well as an overall rating are also presented, the likelihood of misleading ratings will be substantially reduced.

In estimating the implementation feasibility of alternatives it is desirable to use raters who are familiar with the administrative and political environment as well as the program itself.

3. *Analysts or officials might try to develop variations of alternatives that would make implementation more feasible.* This can be done after considering major implementation hurdles. Analysts should not eliminate alternatives because of major obstacles to implementation. Decision makers, not analysts, should decide whether an alternative is worth considering. Thus, the potential costs and effectiveness of major alternatives, even those with substantial apparent implementation difficulties, should be analyzed. Ways to ease implementation of an alternative can often be designed, but attention should be paid to possible added costs and reduced effectiveness introduced.

4. *Program analysis teams should include personnel of the agencies affected, those that will participate in implementation.* Their involvement in the process of analysis should lead to more feasible alternatives and also make findings more palatable by relieving the problem of "not-invented-here."

5. *Analysts might participate in the early stages of implementation.* This will enable the analysts to provide their insights regarding implementation and will give feedback to the analysts on actual implementation problems.

Who Should Do Implementation Feasibility Analysis?

Some jurisdictions may prefer to consider analysis of feasibility completely separate from basic program analysis, perhaps on the assumption that different kinds of personnel are required. This might eliminate one advantage

Exhibit 22.   FEASIBILITY CRITERIA:
               A RATING CHART[a]

Criterion	Current Mode	Option No. 1	Option No. 2	Comments
1. Procurement/personnel regulations				
2. Federal regulations				
3. Agency reaction				
4. Executive Office reaction				
5. Legislature reaction				
6. Public reaction				
7. Personnel dislocation				
8. Political consequences				
9. Personnel availability				
10. Deliverer availability				
11. Need for new facilities				
12. Manager frustration				
13. Employee satisfaction				
14. Competitive environment				
15. Monitoring experience				
16. Corruption				
17. Interrelationships				
18. Workload fluctuations				
19. Occurrence of recent crises				

Source: The Urban Institute and Council of State Governments (July 1987).

a. Suggested rating scale for each option under consideration: major problem, moderate problem, minor problem, no problem, N/A—not applicable, DK—don't know. In the "Comments" column, or on separate pages, give the rationale for the ratings. Use actual quantitative information wherever possible. If quantitative estimates are not available, focus on qualitative comparisons among the options. Rate each option relative to each of the others in each of the criteria.

See appendix D for description of each criterion.

of implementation feasibility analysis, namely alerting program analysts to realistic implications of alternatives. Many, if not most, program analysts are oriented toward quantitative measurement and may feel uncomfortable with the more qualitative analysis of feasibility. However, the systematic approach of the program analyst would be useful in feasibility studies. Feasibility analysis seems particularly appropriate when analyzing major alternative delivery approaches such as contracting out.

Some Final Comments

One problem that could inhibit formal implementation feasibility analysis is the sensitive nature of the analysis itself. Because government analyses inevitably become public, candid implementation information could cause problems among various interest groups. However, if a proper, nonmanipulative tone is used throughout the analysis, this problem can be alleviated.

Chapter 7
Other Analytical Considerations

This chapter discusses five special program analysis topics:

1. Needs assessment—an important ingredient for many analyses
2. Consideration of client difficulty—desirable in most analyses
3. Cost-benefit analysis—a special type of program analysis
4. Determination of the time period that the analysis should cover—necessary in all analyses
5. Need to consider the extent of uncertainty of analysis findings.

Each is discussed below.

Needs Assessment

A major aspect of many program analyses is determining how well an alternative will meet the estimated need for a service. The term "need," however, is vague, implies a variety of meanings, and is difficult to express quantitatively.

In general, analysts must consider both *expressed* demand, based, for example, on the past usage of the particular service, and *latent* (hidden) demand. The latter is the demand that would occur if, for example, citizens were better informed about the program or if changes were made to make the program more accessible or attractive or less expensive for users. The estimation of latent demand can add considerably to the difficulty of program analysis.

The term needs assessment is most often applied in studies of the need for human service programs, such as programs for families with incomes below the poverty line, the homeless, persons with mental health problems, and families with other health and social service needs. However, more often public agencies focus solely on those persons and families that <u>apply</u> for help. Typically because of tight budgets, government agencies do not count those that do not apply, and thus the agency does not conduct needs assessments for nonapplicants.

When human service needs assessments are done, analysts typically use one or more of the following data collection procedures:[1]

• Examination of social and economic data from agency records, such as data on the incidence of various diseases, low-weight births, persons applying for various types of public assistance benefits, unemployment, persons on waiting lists, and so on.

• Surveys of the population, especially those that ask households about the incidence of levels of various problems in the household in order to estimate the incidence of various problems in the community.

• Surveys of key informants in the jurisdiction to obtain a cross-section of "expert" judgment about the incidence and severity of various problems in the jurisdiction.

In most other services, need is indicated by physical measurements such as street condition assessments, water or air pollution measurements, amount of daily water consumption, number of crimes reported, requests for services from citizens, and so on.

These various sources can provide information on the current magnitude of the incidence and prevalence of various problems. To estimate *future* needs, however, analysts must use techniques similar to those discussed in chapter 5, such as statistical projections of past data.

Consideration of Client Difficulty

As noted in chapter 5, many estimates of the effectiveness of a program require estimates to be made of effectiveness for different categories of clients.

---

1. For details on needs assessment procedures see, for example, United Way of America, *COMPASS: Charting Courses for Community Caring*, especially booklet on "Tools for Collecting and Analyzing Data" (Alexandria, Virginia: United Way of America, 1987); and Robert M. Moloney, "Needs Assessment for Human Services," in *Managing Human Services* (Washington, D.C.: International City Management Association, 1977). For discussions of problems and limitations of human service needs assessments see Wayne A. Kimmel, "Needs Assessment: A Critical Perspective" in Ralph M. Kramer and Harry Specht, editors, *Readings in Community Organization Practice* (Englewood Cliffs, New Jersey: Prentice-Hall, 1983); and Russy D. Summarwalla, *Needs Assessment: The State of the Art* (Alexandria, Virginia: United Way of America, 1982).

If the mix of clients is changing, overall effectiveness will be affected. This applies not only to human resource programs, but also in one form or other to most government programs.

For example, an analyst concerned with police programs may use as measures of effectiveness the crime rate and the proportion of cases that are closed by apprehension of suspects. To gain a valid picture, however, the analysts should set up categories of crimes according to their type and severity to distinguish, for example, between robbery and minor vandalism.

The analyst, thus, needs to project how many cases will fall into each category of difficulty and how effective a program will be for each category. The analysis may find important differences both in the resources needed to deal with each category of cases, and in the effectiveness of the various program alternatives in treating each category.

Cost-Benefit Analysis and Other Methods to Combine Effectiveness Measures[2]

Most program analyses use several measures of effectiveness. Because the measures often are in different units, it can be difficult for public officials to decide on the best course of action. For instance, is it worth installing a stop light system that prevents twelve automobile accidents, saves two lives, and prevents four injuries, but adds seventy years of travel time? Should the city allow construction of a plant that will create 500 jobs, if the pollution it generates will cloak the city in haze an additional forty days per year?

These are difficult questions, and they cannot be resolved unless someone implicitly or explicitly judges the trade-off between the disparate effects. Several methods can be used to aid the decision process. The best known is *cost-benefit analysis.*

In cost-benefit analysis, dollar values are inferred or imputed for some or all of the effectiveness measures. Once the effects are restated in terms of estimated monetary benefits, they can be compared directly to dollar costs. If a project's dollar benefits exceed its dollar costs, the project presumably is worthwhile. Furthermore, alternatives can be ranked on a scale showing the ratio of costs to benefits, or a scale showing the dollar value of benefits net of costs.[3]

---

2. This section was prepared by Ted Miller of The Urban Institute.

3. For a basic discussion of cost-benefit analysis see Stokey and Zeckhauser (1978), chapters 9 and 10. For more detailed technical discussions see Dorfman (1965), Gramlich (1981), Mishan (1982), and Musgrove and Musgrove (1984), chapters 8 and 9. (The Dorfman work is old but is a classic containing excellent discussion of ways to impute monetary values for such programs as outdoor recreation, highway investments, and disease control.)

The monetary value of many benefits is not readily estimated, however. Program effects are not commodities like doormats produced in a sheltered workshop that can be valued by looking at how much comparable doormats cost in a store. Instead, the values of these benefits must be inferred, perhaps by estimating how much people are willing to pay to change their rate of occurrence.

Some of the bases that have been used for valuing benefits are (1) the cost of actions that people take to reduce the likelihood of adverse outcomes—for example, home burglar alarm sales give information on the value people place on reducing the risk of crime, while the choice of automobile speed gives insight into the relative values a driver places on travel time and safety; (2) market surrogates—for example, tolls paid to use a fast road indicate how much people are willing to pay for travel time, while the value of recreation time has been estimated from the cost of movie tickets or the amount people pay to travel to the beach and obtain lodging there; (3) the compensation people accept in place of the benefit, such as wage premiums paid to people in risky jobs or court awards to compensate for injury; (4) citizen surveys to determine what people say they are willing to pay for public services; or (5) the subset of costs that are readily measured—for example, lost wages are a lower bound estimate of the value of a life.

Because benefit values are estimates, often controversial ones, we recommend using them only as a *supplement* to the delineation of program effects, and then only if the method for imputing dollar values is clearly presented—so that decision makers can see for themselves the values of the various measures of program effects and can understand the basis for the imputations. Caution also is advisable in comparing the dollar cost and benefit estimates because dollars from different sources are not necessarily the same. Is it appropriate, for example, to decide whether to use tax dollars to build noise barriers along a highway based on a value of noise pollution reduction estimated by comparing the sales prices people pay for similar houses in noisy versus quiet areas? It is unclear that a dollar of public spending has the same implications as a dollar of private spending.

A further shortcoming of many cost-benefit analyses is their failure to identify the effects on different client groups. The effects on selected groups often are of concern from a public policy standpoint. A program in which low-income households bear a disproportionate share of the costs usually is less desirable than a slightly more expensive program that spreads costs more evenly across income groups. Decision makers also generally want to know if program choices will have very different impacts on some age, racial or ethnic groups, or other politically important constituencies.

Some benefit estimates not only are tenuous but quite controversial. Values for life are especially so. Many people view life as sacred; they are offended if the government places a dollar value on life. And although lost earnings sometimes are used to value lives saved in analyses by state and local governments, this approach places little or no value on the lives of children and the elderly.[4]

A useful alternative to valuing all important benefits in dollars is to *convert the benefits to more nearly commensurate units*. For example, the stop light issue mentioned at the start of this section might be described as the trade-off between $12,000 in accident damages to vehicles, 55 years of life, and 8 years of functional impairment versus 70 years of travel time and the $18,000 cost of the stop light system. When phrased in this manner, the policy issue is clearer—are future years of life worth more than current years of travel time?

Units that frequently can be used to capture most effects of a program include time, employment, clients served to a certain standard, and dollars. The cost-effectiveness of alternative approaches then can be compared, for example, in terms of cost per life-year saved or per family adequately housed.

Converting to common units can be risky if it masks important differences in outcomes. A study of a federal motor vehicle safety standard, for example, converted injuries into "equivalent fatality units" using weights based on the relative medical costs and earnings loss associated with deaths and injuries. Implicitly this method assumed that pain and suffering would mirror the economic costs. In reality, however, most people view brain damage and spinal cord injury as fates worse than death, even though they have far lower economic costs. Thus the analysis substantially underestimated the benefits of the safety standard.

Another approach used to guide trade-offs among noncommensurate benefits is to *weight the benefits*, for instance by estimating that curing one case of tranquilizer addiction is half as important as curing a case of cocaine addiction. Common methods for selecting weights are citizen surveys about priorities or use of the Delphi technique to obtain the consensus of experts.[5]

Weighting is inherently arbitrary, although it may provide a politically defensible rationale. When possible, we feel that a reduction in the number of noncommensurate units is a useful first step, even if some implicit or explicit weighting needs to be involved in the decision. For example, if the impacts of tranquilizer and cocaine addiction on such common measures as lost years of productive functioning and number of crimes induced are ex-

---

4. For a more complete discussion of life valuation issues see Brenda Kragh, Ted Miller, and Kenneth Reinert, "Accident Costs for Highway Safety Decisionmaking," *Public Roads*, vol. 50, no. 1, June 1986.

5. See, for example, Sackman (1974).

plicitly accounted for, the choice of which to prevent may become clear without detailed consideration of impacts that cannot be converted to comparable units.

When weighted or collapsed measures are used in an analysis, it is important to treat them as a supplement. The complete list of effects should be presented and the method used to combine them should be described.

Time Period To Be Covered by the Analysis

Analyses that consider only the immediate future, such as the next budget year, often lead to short-sighted decisions. In this respect, it is more desirable to consider costs and effects as far into the future as relevant. On the other hand, the longer the time period involved in the projection, the greater are the uncertainties in the estimates.

How many future years should be considered? Unfortunately, there is little documented guidance on this issue.

The need to consider future years is affected by the extent to which a current decision can be revised at a later date. Analyses of alternatives that involve substantial capital expenditures (such as fire stations, water or sewage treatment plants, and hospitals) have significant long-range implications and are likely to require estimates for perhaps ten or more years. Decisions on procedural matters, such as the deployment of maintenance crews or police patrol units, which do not involve additional staff or facilities, generally require shorter time periods of perhaps two to three years. However, even personnel and procedural changes (such as those in which substantial increases in personnel are required or where new program constituencies are likely to form rapidly) are at times difficult to reverse or alter. A longer planning horizon may then be needed.

The program analyst should consider how long it will take to procure the resources for each alternative, how long it will take to implement the program once resources are in place, and how long the program will operate. A reasonable length of time should be allowed. For example, in the analysis of a drug treatment program summarized in appendix A-3, analysts looked at the effectiveness of the program over five years. This allowed for start-up time—hiring staff, obtaining a facility, and attracting and selecting patients—and for the program to stabilize so that cost and effectiveness data would properly reflect the impact on clients in various phases of treatment.

Generally the time period for any projection should be long enough so that costs and long-term benefits stabilize or reach a recurring cycle. If decision makers are likely to be concerned about the cost of an initial investment, the analysis should cover the time likely to be needed to pay back the investment. For some program options, such as an extension of an existing program, this may be only one or two years. For those involving new programs with new concepts or new construction, this may be at least five or ten years.

The length of the projected time period should also allow for a consideration of possible significant changes in conditions that could alter the attractiveness of an alternative. A key question often will be how long it will take for the alternative to become obsolete because of new technologies or a change in clients. For example, projected rates of community growth could alter the need for various public facilities. Obviously, this should be considered in making current facility decisions. In a fire station location analysis, for example, analysts constructed a model with the city configured as the planners projected it for ten years as well as for the current period. Investment and operating costs were considered for each alternative.[6]

Some "future" considerations are occasionally overlooked in program analyses:

1. New facilities and equipment carry maintenance costs. Estimated savings may be overstated if future maintenance costs, particularly those for complex new facilities or equipment, are not considered.

2. It usually takes time for new programs to shake down and become fully operational. Estimates of near-future program performance are likely to be overstated if this start-up phase is not considered.

3. Programs that involve personnel reductions are likely to encounter delays before full savings are realized. Personnel reductions can be achieved through attrition or transfers rather than by dismissals.

4. The effects of future inflation on salaries, costs of equipment, and prices of land may considerably escalate program costs, especially for items that involve extended lead time. This is especially important where program options involve different phasing or mixes of cost items with differing inflation factors.

5. Demand or need for a program may change in the future, as may the types of clients to be served.

---

6. International City Management Association, *Applying Systems Analysis in Urban Government: Three Case Studies* (Washington, D.C., March 1972).

Considering Uncertainty

Estimates of future conditions under which programs will operate, of future program effectiveness, and of future program costs are inherently uncertain. Use of sound techniques and the best available data should improve the quality of estimates. But by no means will this remove uncertainty.

A program analysis should identify major uncertainties and, to the extent feasible, identify their magnitudes and implications for program decisions. This will require careful consideration of the linkage between proposed program features and program effectiveness and cost. Unfortunately, very few program analyses specifically identify and estimate the extent to which uncertainties are present in findings. The problem can be illustrated by an employment training example. Training does not automatically lead to employment. Estimating only the number of people completing training is not sufficient. Estimates also are needed as to the likely availability of jobs at the time training is completed in those occupations for which training is aimed. Assumptions about economic and job market conditions—which have their own uncertainties—also would be required.

The analytical problems and available alternatives for estimating and handling uncertainty are in themselves a major and lengthy topic. Some approaches that might be used include the following:

1. Providing estimates of the probabilities of various events or conditions. Depending on the degree of uncertainty, these estimates could be expressed in a precise manner or in qualitative statements of the degree of likelihood.

2. Estimating how much the results will change in response to possible changes in major assumptions used in the analysis ("sensitivity analysis"). Analysts would appraise the likely influence on cost and effectiveness estimates for each alternative of different assumptions, particularly those subject to major uncertainty.

3. Expressing estimates of cost and effectiveness with ranges of values rather than a single value. Ranges might be based on the following:[7]

---

7. This effort can become quite technically sophisticated. For example, some efforts have been made to obtain quantitative estimates of the "highest likely," "most likely," and "least likely" values for individual cost or effectiveness elements from experts. Based on assumed probability distributions for the actual values of each element (such as the Beta distribution used for PERT estimates in scheduling), all these elements would then be combined into total cost or effectiveness estimates. This would produce an expected value and "confidence intervals" for the totals.

(a) statistical calculations where statistical sampling is used;

(b) calculations obtained by altering the values of various variables based on information available to the analysts (especially feasible when computerized mathematical models have been used to help make estimates of costs and effectiveness);

(c) expert judgment.

4. At the very least, providing qualitative statements about major uncertainties and risks involved.

Information about the magnitude of uncertainty in the analytical findings is valuable in the following ways:

First, it warns those using the results about the risks in selecting each program alternative. One of the few examples where uncertainty is often explicitly considered quantitatively in government services occurs in decisions on water supply and drainage facilities. Probabilities of various amounts of rainfall are calculated (based on historical records) and often expressed in such terms as a "once-every-hundred-years rain." The likelihood and risks that various facility capacities will be too small can then be calculated. Decision makers can then make their choices based on the costs and risks involved.

Second, government officials may want to select those alternatives that hold up well under a range of possible "futures" (termed "robust" alternatives), rather than accept an alternative that might perform extremely well under one possible set of conditions but poorly under other possible conditions. Such information may also encourage the development of new alternatives as "hedges" against major uncertainties.

Third, if program selection involves inordinate uncertainty and risk, this factor may suggest the need for better, less uncertain information—perhaps by more extensive data collection or by undertaking pilot projects—prior to final decisions.

Many analysts warn against presenting findings without providing adequate information about the nature and degree of uncertainty present in findings. Unfortunately, this problem continues to be neglected. Time and resource constraints, the desire of users for simple, easy-to-grasp findings, and technical difficulties in making additional estimates conspire to discourage the explicit consideration of uncertainty. In the face of such realities, we suggest that each program analysis be required to contain, at a minimum, a statement of the nature and magnitude of uncertainties, even if it is only a brief paragraph about the degree to which a user can have confidence in the figures presented.

Chapter 8
Three Major Applications for Program Analysis

Three important continuing applications of program analysis exist for most state and local governments.[1] Program analysis can and probably should be used in the following contexts:

1. Examining opportunities for improving the *productivity* of specific government programs and services.
2. Considering the potential costs and benefits of *alternative service delivery* approaches, such as contracting with the private sector.
3. Making choices about *capital facility* improvements and maintenance.

Each application is discussed below.

Productivity Improvement Analysis

Claims of wastefulness abound at all levels of government. Improving the efficiency and productivity of government services is a concern and obligation of all government agencies. Yet only a few state and local governments have established formal, government-wide productivity improvement programs. Some governments and some individual operating agencies, however, have management analysis offices that occasionally do productivity studies. The impacts of individual productivity improvement studies on a government may be modest, but when a number are done, the impacts can cumulate over the years and provide substantial cost savings and quality

---

1. Appendix A contains three specific, detailed examples of basic program analysis.

improvements. Productivity improvement analysis can use many of the principles of program analysis. In fact, productivity improvement analysis can be considered as a type of program analysis.

A typical focus of state and local productivity improvement programs is the examination of the government work force to determine if the number of activities can be reduced or "rearranged." Productivity analyses typically examine how much time each activity should take and what future workloads are likely to be for each task. The estimated workload is then multiplied by the amount of time each task should take, and staffing required for the estimated projected workload is then calculated. Adjustments are made for "down-time" (such as rest breaks, holidays, vacations, and sick leave).

Such studies often have two limiting deficiencies: first, the analysis does not explicitly consider the end objectives of the work and the quality needed, but rather focuses on narrow cost reduction and efficiency objectives; and second, the analysis considers only current work procedures, excluding examination of better ways to do the work or of whether some or all of the work tasks are actually needed.

Productivity studies are, in effect, program analyses. They should include these explicit steps:

1. Identify objectives of the work activity and corresponding criteria to assess whether the objectives are being met. Evaluation criteria should include not only cost (expressed both in terms of work hours and dollars), the usual primary focus of such studies, but should also explicitly cover service quality.

2. Examine the current cost and level of quality of the service activity.

3. Based on this evidence and on observations of the way the current activity is being performed, identify alternative ways to do the activity—including eliminating tasks no longer needed and considering new procedures to do the work in different ways. (The next section of this chapter discusses more radical alternatives such as substantially changing the delivery system by, for example, switching to contracting. This section concentrates on internal improvements.)

4. Assess the cost and service quality effects of each alternative. Although uncertainties and risks should be examined, they are not likely to be as important as in capital facility decisions, which have effects several years into the future, and which may require mid-term adjustments that are expensive or difficult.

An exemplary productivity improvement analysis of a library system was conducted by Dade County, Florida. In the summary that follows, we note that concern over the quality of the service to its clients, such as accessibility to citizens, was an important issue for the Dade library system.[2]

The library productivity improvement analysis began when the manager of the Dade County Office of Productivity Management (OPM) ordered a review and revision of current staffing levels and hours of operation of the county's libraries. The analysis was precipitated by a Library Department budget request for a number of additional full-time and part-time positions. The analysis included the steps outlined below.

1. Interviews with library division heads to determine the activities performed by library staff.

2. Estimates of time required for each task based on employee reports. (A more reliable procedure would be to use engineering time and motion study techniques. OPM used the latter procedures to estimate times for the patron-assistance activity.)

3. Collection of data on the quantity of major library activities such as the number of materials circulated, materials reshelved, desk and telephone patron assistance requests, programs (by type), and patron counts. In each case, data were sought by hour, day, and week.

4. A joint survey of library patrons by the Library Department and OPM. It was administered for a two-week period in each library. A questionnaire was given to each patron who came to one of the libraries to complete on a voluntary basis. Patrons were asked about their preferences for hours and days of operation, satisfaction with the availability and quality of staff service, satisfaction with the quality and quantity of materials in the libraries, and satisfaction with the quality and quantity of programs for adults and children.

5. Telephone interviews with selected library systems elsewhere in the country to obtain suggestions about other options including schedules of operation, organization structures, and methods for determining staffing levels. Contacts with other jurisdictions were not used to obtain data on costs, service quality, or implementation feasibility. Information from one library system (on circulation standards, that is, annual circulation per full-time equivalent employee) was used to help derive staffing needs for Dade County's circulation activity.

---

2. This description is based on Dade County Office of Productivity Management, "Library Department Productivity Analysis Study Final Report," Dade County, Miami, Florida, May 1985, supplemented by conversations with OPM staff.

The OPM/library team used information from the analysis of quantity of activities by time during the week (the third step above), and from the patron survey (the fourth step) to develop recommendations about the hours each library should be open. This resulted in recommendations to shift the hours of many libraries. Some would open somewhat later in the morning and close somewhat later in the afternoon. All libraries would be open on Saturdays with some closing on Sundays and Mondays. Overall this would result in a net increase of 43.5 hours of library operation each week, the equivalent of one new branch library.

Based on the information obtained from the procedures identified above, the OPM/library team also made specific staffing recommendations, which in total called for one less full-time and thirty-two fewer part-time employees than the Library Department's budget request and $245,000 net savings. The analysts noted in their report that the added hours of library time would cost about $330,000 per year. Thus the total of the actual dollar savings plus the cost avoided for the added library time gives a total value of the proposed alternative of $575,000 per year. The analysis recommendations were accepted and implemented by the county.

Examination of Alternative Service Delivery Approaches Such as Contracting

Since 1978, when tax containment efforts received a powerful impetus from Proposition 13 in California, governments at all levels have given much greater consideration to service delivery options other than direct delivery by government employees. A list of options, with brief definitions, is presented in exhibit 23. Alternatives such as these should be considered when examining a program along with internal improvements that might be made to an existing program.

During 1986 and 1987 seven operating departments in the states of Maryland and Delaware compared the current delivery approach of one of their programs with other delivery approaches. Exhibit 24 summarizes the programs and alternatives.

Estimate of Impacts

Analysts examining alternative delivery approaches will likely have special problems estimating the impacts of major alternatives, especially when the alternatives involve delivery approaches with which the government agency is not familiar. If the approach is new, data can be sought on experiences

Exhibit 23. DEFINITIONS OF ALTERNATIVE SERVICE
DELIVERY APPROACHES

1. *Contracting out/purchase of service.* The government contracts with private firms (profit or nonprofit) to provide goods or deliver services. The government may contract to have all, or a portion, of a service provided by the private firm.

2. *Franchises.* The government awards either an exclusive or non-exclusive franchise to private firms to provide a service within a certain geographical area. Under a franchise agreement, the citizen directly pays the firm for the service.

3. *Grants/subsidies.* The government makes a financial or in-kind contribution to a private organization or individuals to encourage them to provide a service so that the government does not have to provide it.

4. *Vouchers.* The government provides vouchers to citizens needing the service. The citizens are then free to choose the organization from which to obtain the goods or services. The citizen gives the voucher to the organization, which obtains reimbursement from the government.

5. *Volunteers.* Individuals in the jurisdictions provide free help to a government agency. This approach, as defined here, is limited to volunteers that work directly for a government. It does not include individuals doing volunteer work for a private (for example, charitable) agency.

6. *Self-help.* The government encourages individuals or groups, such as neighborhood or community associations, to undertake for their own benefit activities that the government would otherwise have to undertake.

Exhibit 23. (continued)

7. *Use of regulatory and taxing authority.* The government uses its regulatory (deregulatory) or taxing authority to encourage private sector organizations or individuals to provide a service, or at least to reduce the need for public services.

8. *User fees and charges to adjust demand.* Users of a service are charged a fee based on how much they use the government-supplied activity, thus putting the fiscal burden on users of the activity. For the purposes here, we are not concerned with the use of fees and charges for the sake of raising revenues.

9. *Encouraging private organizations to take over an activity ("divestiture").* Here the government actually gives up responsibility for an activity but works with a private agency (profit or nonprofit) willing to take over responsibility. This might involve a one-time grant or subsidy.

10. *Reducing demand for service ("de-marketing").* The government attempts to reduce the need and demand for a government service through a variety of "marketing" techniques.

11. *Obtaining temporary help from private firms.* Private firms loan personnel, facilities, or equipment, or even provide funds to the government.

12. *Joint public-private ventures.* Businesses and the government join forces for a major development, such as a new economic development or revitalization project.

13. *Internal productivity improvements.* The government takes strictly internal actions to make better use of its existing resources—to reduce its costs for a given level of output or increase output (quantity or quality) for a given expenditure level. Numerous approaches to productivity improvement exist, such as use of new technology, employee motivational programs, work methods changes, and organizational changes.

Source: Adapted from Harry P. Hatry, *A Review of Private Approaches to the Delivery of Public Services* (Washington, D.C.: The Urban Institute, 1983).

Exhibit 24.   LIST OF MARYLAND AND DELAWARE SERVICE
DELIVERY PROJECTS

MARYLAND

Department of General Services

Snow removal at the nine state multiservice center lots. Currently done at
eight of the centers by contractors. The focus was to compare the current
approach to the option of state employee delivery.

Department of Education

Vocational education of inmates at the three Hagerstown correctional facilities for adult males—medium security institutions. Currently vocational
education is provided by state employees with a small amount of contracting
to the community college and some arrangements with individual private
instructors. Options to expand the amount of contracting or to return to
total state employee delivery were examined.

Psychological diagnostic examinations for prospective clients of vocational
rehabilitation programs. Currently the vocational rehabilitation program is
required to rotate the examinations among all licensed practitioners who
wish to be on the state's list. The group examined contracting to organizations and agreements with other government agencies.

Department of Health and Mental Hygiene

Monitoring the performance of community-based private residential and
nonresidential programs for juveniles. Currently state employees do a limited amount of monitoring. The group examined a variety of ways to
provide the needed, expanded amount of monitoring, including contracting
to private organizations, use of volunteers along with state staff, fran-
chising/licensing of private monitoring organizations, and expansion of
state staff.

Department of Human Resources

Post-adoption services for adoptive families. The group examined a spectrum of approaches such as contracting, more use of self-help, dissemi-
nation of information by the state agency, and use of vouchers.

Income maintenance record keeping. The group considered various technologies and types of contracts with private firms to do such activities as
microfilming and storage of old records.

Exhibit 24. (continued)

DELAWARE

Department of Health and Social Services

Management and operation of five state-operated health-related residential care institutions—public health, mental retardation, and mental health. Options examined by the group included contracting, the creation of a quasi-public corporation, and ways to reduce current rigidities (for example, personnel problems, limitations on management flexibility, and support services).

Department of Corrections

Food services in the seven principal correctional institutions, which are currently provided by state corrections department employees with inmate participation. Options examined included contracting, using volunteers in selected circumstances, and improvements to the current system (such as the use of new "cook-chill" technology).

Department of Administrative Services

Fleet maintenance for state passenger vehicles. Currently each department handles its own maintenance. Some agencies use mostly state employees, some mostly private firms. Options examined included various competitively bid statewide maintenance agreements, and changes in the current delivery arrangement, especially various degrees of centralization and increasing the capacity of state-operated maintenance facilities (such as the Department of Corrections). The group also examined the desirability of installing a management information system (MIS) to track vehicle maintenance costs.

Sources: State of Maryland, "A Process for Periodic Reviews of Alternative Ways to Deliver State Services" (Annapolis, Maryland: Maryland Department of Budget and Fiscal Planning, 1987); and The Urban Institute and the Council of State Governments, "Findings and Recommendations on a Process for the Analysis of Service Delivery Alternatives" (Wilmington, Delaware: State of Delaware Office of State Planning and Coordination, July 1987).

with these alternatives in other governments. For example, if the government is considering contracting for a service for the first time, the analysts can seek information on costs, service quality, and implementation feasibility from jurisdictions that are already contracting for the service.

The Delaware Department of Corrections in 1987 examined the possibility of contracting for inmate food service for its correctional facilities. It surveyed all fifty states and subsequently undertook telephone interviews with ten state correctional agencies that were either currently contracting for inmate food service or that had contracted in the past but terminated contract operation. Analysts obtained cost data, qualitative information on service quality, and information on problems that had occurred and ways such problems had been alleviated.

Similarly, the Delaware Department of Administrative Services sponsored a telephone survey to identify states that had implemented statewide passenger vehicle maintenance contracting, with the objective of obtaining feedback from these states on costs, service quality, and problems encountered.[3]

Comparisons of alternatives involving substantially different delivery approaches may have to include a substantial *qualitative* element. In these cases analysts should at a minimum make qualitative judgments of the likely relative levels of each cost and service quality criterion. The analysts provide the reasoning for their qualitative ratings just as they record in their reports the sources of data they use when presenting *quantitative* information.

A government may be able to take some initial steps to obtain pertinent information, particularly on costs, to reduce the analysts' dependence on qualitative judgments. For contracting options, for example, a government might issue a preliminary request-for-qualifications to determine whether enough supplies are available to provide an adequate level of competitive bidding.

Another major problem that government analysts are likely to face, but one considerably more correctable, is lack of information on the quality of the existing program. All too often such information is missing for state and local programs. All seven Delaware and Maryland state agencies found this to be the case in the analyses they undertook in 1986 and 1987 to examine alternative service delivery approaches. In each instance teams had to attempt to develop such information themselves. For example, the Maryland team

---

3. Both these Delaware examples are reported in The Urban Institute and Council of State Governments, "Findings and Recommendations on a Process for the Analysis of Service Delivery Alternatives" (Wilmington, Delaware: State of Delaware Office of State Planning and Coordination, July 1987).

that examined its vocational rehabilitation and psychological screening program undertook a special survey of a sample of recent examination reports and asked its field staff to rate the quality and timeliness of each report—as a baseline for comparing other, modified, delivery methods. The Delaware team that examined food services for inmates in state prisons prepared a food rating form and rated a sample of the food in each of its major correctional facilities to give the team a perspective on the quality of food under the current delivery system.

The Maryland Department of General Services team compared its current approach to snow removal at state facilities (contracting for the service) to the possibility of switching back to snow removal by state employees. To obtain data on the quality of the current contracting approach, the team examined department records for the previous four years on calls by the department to the contractors requesting snow removal.

The problem of inadequate data on the quality of existing programs is not unique to the analysis of "privatization" approaches. Analysts usually have to develop their own data on program quality; adequate data will not likely be readily available.

Consideration of Implementation Feasibility

Analysis of innovative options, such as various privatization options, should give special attention to implementation feasibility. Most shifts in service delivery approach are bound to entail major barriers to successful implementation. Such barriers include restrictive laws and regulations, objections from employees and their associations or unions, concerns of clients who are apprehensive about new service arrangements, and the like.

Appendix D presents a list of implementation feasibility criteria that were used by the seven Maryland and Delaware state agency study teams as part of their analyses of privatization alternatives. (Exhibit 22 in chapter 6 shows the "IF" rating chart and scale that some of those agencies used in their analyses.)

As indicated in chapter 6, this IF analysis not only indicates the extent of feasibility but also can be used to suggest modifications to individual alternatives that will ease some implementation obstacles, such as adding an extra low-cost service to help clients accept the change. This type of analysis will also indicate whether added costs are likely to accrue to particular alternatives (such as added procurement costs due to delays in implementation or additional costs for helping displaced employees), or whether diminished program effectiveness is likely (due to the need to alter some part of the new approach in order to gain its acceptance)—thus making the emphasis more realistic.

Displaying the Results

Of major importance to making the results of analysis useful is the way analysts present their findings. Analysts (whether government, university, or others) often write poorly. They often do not organize their report material so that readers can follow the report's logic easily, and do not make sufficient use of visual aids, such as summary tables and charts, to help the reader quickly identify key findings. Exhibit 25 provides an example of an effective graphic summary presentation used by the Delaware Department of Health and Social Services to brief high-level state officials. The exhibit summarizes the analysts' conclusions about each of three alternative arrangements for operation of state nursing homes. (See exhibit 24 for more information on the study.) A key feature of this presentation is that it highlights direct comparisons among the options on each of the three overall characteristics that the analysts examined: efficiency (cost), service quality, and implementation feasibility. The exhibit was based on the more detailed findings presented in the body of the final report.

Analysis of Capital Improvement and Maintenance Alternatives

State and local governments make decisions annually about which projects they will support in the forthcoming budget year to maintain existing capital facilities (infrastructure). Bridges collapse; water mains break; sewers overflow; roads fill with potholes—all of which can create nightmares for public officials. Governments should make their decisions so that (1) the costs to the public are as low as possible, (2) the facilities provide high-quality needed services, and (3) the allocations are distributed reasonably equitably among various parts of the community.

Major items of infrastructure include roads, bridges, water supply and wastewater distribution and treatment facilities, solid waste disposal facilities, and public buildings. Government agencies must decide which particular *capital* projects should be funded and which actions should be taken to provide ongoing *maintenance*. Every state and local government annually makes these decisions (most of which are implicit rather than explicit) for components of its infrastructure (for instance, for each block of road pavement, each section of water pipe, each bridge, each building, and so on). The decisions relate to whether the component should be replaced, rehabilitated, repaired only if some problem occurs, or given some form of preventive maintenance.

Illuminating these choices is a basic task of program analysis.

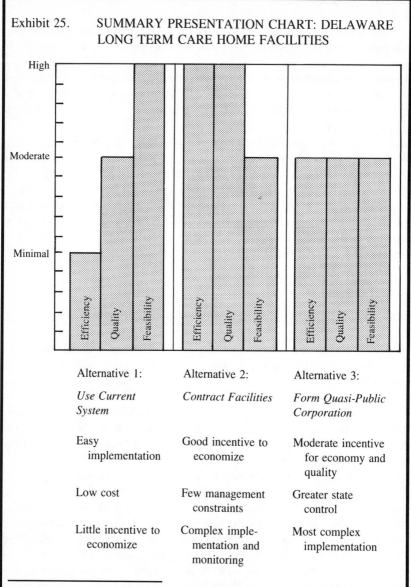

Exhibit 25. SUMMARY PRESENTATION CHART: DELAWARE LONG TERM CARE HOME FACILITIES

Alternative 1:

Use Current System

Easy implementation

Low cost

Little incentive to economize

Alternative 2:

Contract Facilities

Good incentive to economize

Few management constraints

Complex implementation and monitoring

Alternative 3:

Form Quasi-Public Corporation

Moderate incentive for economy and quality

Greater state control

Most complex implementation

Source: Delaware Department of Health and Social Services, paper entitled "Alternative Service Delivery," submitted to Delaware Governor's Management Improvement Committee, July 16, 1987.

Governments usually do not use formal program analysis to make their choices. Rather, the most frequent approach is a combination of "repairing only if a problem arises (crisis maintenance)," perhaps combined with the strategy of "repairing only those components of the infrastructure in the worst condition." Explicit consideration of the value of preventive maintenance is seldom done. Capital budgets are usually decided more often by how many dollars a government believes are available than by calculations about whether the costs of specific projects are "worth it," taking into account estimates of future savings or improved service quality, or both.

The concepts and practices of program analysis can be used at each of three levels of decision:

1. the type of maintenance to be applied to specific infrastructure *components* (replacement, rehabilitation, repair or preventive maintenance);
2. the projects that should be given priority within a specific service *area* (which streets, bridges, pipe sections, facilities, and so on)
3. the setting of priorities among classes of projects (for instance, whether a street project or a water project should be funded) and determination of how many projects should be funded.

Objectives and Evaluation Criteria

Service quality criteria can be identified for each particular service area and, more generally, for all service areas. Exhibit 26 presents a general set of evaluation criteria that can be used to compare projects proposed by different departments (the third level listed above). A rating system such as that used by the City of Dayton, Ohio (see exhibit 27) can be used to compare candidate projects. (The rating categories illustrated, however, should be defined more concretely, and in quantitative terms whenever possible.)

When projects or types of maintenance within a service area are compared (the second level listed above), more specific evaluation criteria are needed for each particular service area. For example, for roads and bridges the objectives of capital maintenance and replacement decisions involve assuring safety, moving traffic as rapidly as possible, and providing a comfortable ride for travelers. Safety can be measured in terms of accident and injury rates. Traffic times can be measured directly. Road conditions can be evaluated in terms of their roughness. The structural condition of bridges can be periodically assessed. Values for the measures of these systems can be ob-

Exhibit 26.   SUGGESTED CAPITAL INVESTMENT
EVALUATION CRITERIA

1. Fiscal impacts (on costs and revenues)

2. Health and safety effects

3. Community economic effects

4. Environmental, aesthetic, and social effects

5. Amount of disruption and inconvenience caused by the project

6. Distributional effects—who is affected and how

7. Feasibility, including public support and project readiness

8. Implications of deferring the project

9. Amount of uncertainty and risk

10. Effects on interjurisdictional relationships

11. Advantages accruing from relationship to other capital proposals

Source: Hatry, Harry P.; Millar, Annie P.; and Evans, James H., *Guide to Setting Priorities for Capital Investment* (Washington, D.C.: The Urban Institute Press, 1984), page 9.

tained by a number of techniques, including visual ratings by inspectors and mechanical devices (such as ''road meters'' and ''roughmeters'' that measure vertical displacement, or bumpiness, of roads).

For water and sewer systems, evaluation criteria are not as well established, but some criteria measuring the following have been used: the quality of water, water pressure (which can diminish greatly as corrosion accumulates inside pipes), leak history, frequency and severity of sewer backups, extent of corrosion, frequency of interruptions of service, and number of water main breaks.

In all cases, cost is a major criterion in project selection. When dealing with capital facility decisions, it is particularly important to consider long-range, life-cycle costs, not merely costs for the next year or two. An initial investment cost—such as procurement of more reliable construction materials

Exhibit 27. CAPITAL PROJECT RATING FORM, DAYTON, OHIO

MEMBER'S NAME _____

PROJECT NAME _____ NO. _____

	SCORE RANGE	RATER'S SCORE
A. Impact on Dayton's goal of increasing neighborhood vitality		
_____ Major impact	8–10	
_____ Moderate impact	4–7	
_____ Minor impact	1–3	
_____ No impact	0	_____
B. Impact on Dayton's goal of increasing economic vitality		
_____ Major impact	8–10	
_____ Moderate impact	4–7	
_____ Minor impact	1–3	
_____ No impact	0	_____
C. Impact on Dayton's goal of urban conservation		
_____ Major impact	8–10	
_____ Moderate impact	4–7	
_____ Minor impact	1–3	
_____ No impact	0	_____
D. Conformance with plans		
_____ Major element	8–10	
_____ Moderate element	4–7	
_____ Minor element	1–3	
_____ No element	0	_____
E. Priority board ranking		
_____ First priority	10	
_____ Second priority	8	
_____ Third priority	6	
_____ Fourth priority	4	
_____ Fifth priority	2	_____
F. Departmental priority classification		
_____ Critical	9–10	
_____ Valuable	7–8	
_____ Beneficial	5–6	
_____ Desirable	1–4	
_____ Questionable	0	_____

Exhibit 27. (continued)

G. This project directly supports existing
development efforts
    _____ In the Inner Ring   6–10
    _____ Outside the Inner Ring   1–8
    _____ Does not support development efforts   0   _____

H. Impact on expenditures
    _____ Major decrease   6–10
    _____ Minor decrease   1–5
    _____ Remains the same   0
    _____ Increases   −1/−5   _____

I. Impact on energy consumption
    _____ Major reduction   6–10
    _____ Moderate/minor reduction   1–5
    _____ No impact on energy consumption   0
    _____ Increases energy consumption   −1/−5   _____

J. This project is specifically included in an
approved replacement/maintenance schedule
    _____ Yes   6–10
    _____ No   0   _____

K. Impact on economic/redevelopment plan
    _____ Major impact   8–10
    _____ Moderate impact   4–7
    _____ Minor impact   1–3
    _____ No impact   0   _____

L. Project duplicates other available public or private
facility
    _____ Yes   −1/−5
    _____ No   0   _____

M. Rater's general appraisal
                                                       0–10   _____
                                        TOTAL SCORE _____

PROJECT NOTES:

_____

    Source: Hatry, Millar, and Evans, *Guide to Setting Priorities for Capital Investment*, pp. 20–21.

and procedures—may greatly reduce future maintenance and repair costs, as well as reduce future service quality problems, so as to justify the investment cost.

Alternatives

Identifying alternatives is a vital part of program analysis for infrastructure projects. The specific alternatives to be considered depend on the level of analysis; that is, whether the analysis is being done from the perspective of the type of maintenance to be applied to particular components of the infrastructure, the projects within a particular service area to be undertaken, or the priorities to be set among service areas.

As noted earlier, state and local governments often base cutoffs for capital infrastructure projects primarily on perceived annual funding limitations. That is, a cutoff point is established below which additional projects will not be funded. Program analysis could be used to help officials decide where cutoff points should be set, depending on whether individual projects have enough value (such as in reduced future-year costs and improvements in service quality) to be worth current expenditures, even though they would require additional fund-raising by the jurisdiction.

Consideration of Uncertainty and Risk

Infrastructure choices usually affect infrastructure for many years into the future. The need to consider uncertainties, and the risks involved with such uncertainties, can become a major concern in making choices relating to infrastructure maintenance. For example, the length of life and serviceability of particular materials and procedures used to maintain, repair, or construct particular types of facilities can be quite uncertain. Information on the size of the future load (for instance, demand) on the infrastructure component is also very important for making choices and can be subject to considerable uncertainty. The amount of traffic and maximum vehicle loads, for example, are important factors that affect the length of life of road surfaces. The quality and composition of incoming water are key determinants of water treatment facility needs. And the expected size of rain storms and runoffs are key determinants of necessary storm drainage facilities.

Analysts should explicitly consider the probability and consequences (risks) if loads occur that are larger than the designed loads. Computer spreadsheet programs are excellent tools for considering uncertainty using sensitivity analysis. The public agency should balance, on one hand, the costs of defending against risks and, on the other, the consequences if capacities are exceeded.

Consideration of Client Groups

The choice of projects for capital budgets and capital improvement programs is likely to affect individual segments of the community differently. Some projects have a greater effect on specific segments of the community, such as downtown businesses or particular urban, suburban, or rural areas. Some activities may have a negative impact on certain groups such as minorities in the community, for example, by tearing up or disrupting their neighborhoods, or a positive effect, by improving the physical condition of neighborhoods. As indicated in item 6 of the suggested evaluation criteria in exhibit 26, "distributional effects," the distributional effects of each proposed capital project should be explicitly considered.

Three Examples[4]

1. Dallas analysis of repair versus replacement for water mains. The Dallas Department of Water Utilities has regularly used economic analysis to determine whether it should repair or replace particular sections of its water mains. The analysts have developed a standard procedure for this analysis based on the frequency of pipe breaks over the most recent four years (used to estimate the likely future frequency of breaks if the main is not replaced), the latest estimated costs per foot of pipe to repair, and the cost per foot to replace the pipe. The department includes estimates of the time value of money in its calculations and considers a time period of twenty years in its comparisons of repair versus replacement costs. To implement this procedure, the department must maintain accurate records on the incidence of water main breaks. The procedure itself is standardized so that the actual analysis for any given water main segment can be made easily and quickly once the latest data on breaks and costs have been obtained. If the water situation changes substantially in part of the community, such as a major increase in the number of households served by a water main. This procedure would need to be modified.

---

4. Extracted from Harry P. Hatry and Bruce G. Steinthal, *Guide to Selecting Maintenance Strategies for Capital Facilities* (Washington, D.C.: The Urban Institute, 1984), chapter 5. That report also presents a number of other examples of the application of program analysis to infrastructure decisions.

2. State of Minnesota bridge maintenance cost-benefit analysis. An example of how a more systematic approach can alter "intuitive" choice is provided by the State of Minnesota's Department of Transportation.[5] To establish priorities for bridge repair, the department used the state's bridge condition assessment procedures to categorize bridge decks into four deterioration categories based on the percentage of deteriorated concrete: "slight" (less than 5 percent), "moderate" (5 to 20 percent), "severe" (20 to 40 percent), and "critical" (more than 40 percent). The department also categorized the bridges by average daily traffic, using three categories (greater than 10,000 vehicles, 2,000 to 10,000 vehicles, and less than 2,000 vehicles). These categories yielded twelve possible categories of bridges.

A simplified form of cost-benefit analysis was used to help establish funding priorities among these twelve categories. The analysis considered the maintenance cost and the increased life expectancy of the bridge deck. As expected, the analysis determined that the heavily traveled bridge decks with critical deterioration had the highest priorities. Of surprise to the priority-setting task force, however, was that the bridges with slight deterioration (in both of the higher traffic categories) came next. The priority assignments are shown in exhibit 28. The findings confirmed the old adage that "an ounce of prevention was in fact worth a pound of cure. If a deck was in excellent condition with only a minimum amount of chloride contamination, then why not protect it from further salting and eventual deterioration by adding an additional two inches of special concrete?"

3. Utah Department of Transportation examination of impact of deferred maintenance. A classic analysis is the examination by the Utah Department of Transportation of the most cost-effective frequency of pavement rehabilitation (overlays) for state roads.[6] The analysis, in effect, also provides information on the consequences of deferring road maintenance. The state had been funding pavement overlays on the average once every twenty-seven years. Strategy D in exhibit 29 represents the typical 1977 Utah pavement

5. Minnesota Department of Highways, "1976 Report on Policy for Production of Concrete Bridge Decks" (Bridge Deck Task Force, Office of Bridges and Structures, January 15, 1976); Robert G. Tracy, "Priority Assignment of Bridge Deck Repairs" (State of Minnesota Department of Transportation Research and Development Section, 1978); and Robert G. Tracy, "Scheduling the Bridge Deck Repair Program," Public Works, January 1980.

6. This discussion is based primarily on National Cooperative Highway Research Program, "Synthesis 58: Consequences of Deferred Maintenance" (Washington, D.C.: Transportation Research Board, 1981); Peterson, "Good Roads Cost Less" (Utah Department of Transportation, R&D Unit, October 1977); and Peterson, "Keynote Address," in *Proceedings of the Pavement Management Workshop*, Report FHWA-TS-79-206 (Washington, D.C.: U.S. Federal Highway Administration, August 1978).

Exhibit 28.   PRIORITY ASSIGNMENT FOR BRIDGE REPAIR,
              MINNESOTA DEPARTMENT OF
              TRANSPORTATION

		Average Daily Traffic (Number of Vehicles)		
Deck Deterioration *(Percent Unsound Concrete)*		*Greater than 10,000*	*2,000 to 10,000*	*Less than 2,000*
Slight	(0–5)	3	4	10
Moderate	(5–20)	6	7	11
Severe	(20–40)	8	9	12
Critical	(>40)	1	2	5

Source: Adapted from Tracy, "Scheduling the Bridge Deck Repair Program," January 1980.

situation. The pavement is overlaid when the road condition PSI deteriorates to approximately 1.9. (The Utah Present Serviceability Index (PSI) is an index of the quality of the pavement determined by obtaining physical measurements of road condition using a "roadmeter.")

Utah compared this current system to three alternative strategies. These strategies require rehabilitation (overlay) earlier: when the pavement reaches a PSI of 3.0, 2.5 (the "design level" recommended for the highways), and 2.0. These three strategies would require overlays at an average of every seventeen, twenty, and twenty-three years, respectively—as shown in exhibit 29 for strategies A, B, and C. The Utah analysts estimated the costs for each alternative and compared them to the costs of existing practice—strategy D. As pavement deteriorates to a poorer condition, additional effort and cost is required to reinstate its condition. A transportation agency can derive curves such as those in exhibit 29 by analyzing the condition of road surfaces at various times after major repairs have been made.

Exhibit 30 shows the results of this analysis. For each type of road system (primary, secondary, and urban), the total annual maintenance and rehabilitation cost decreased as the frequency of rehabilitation increased. The costs decreased for each type of road system by about 40 percent when the interval

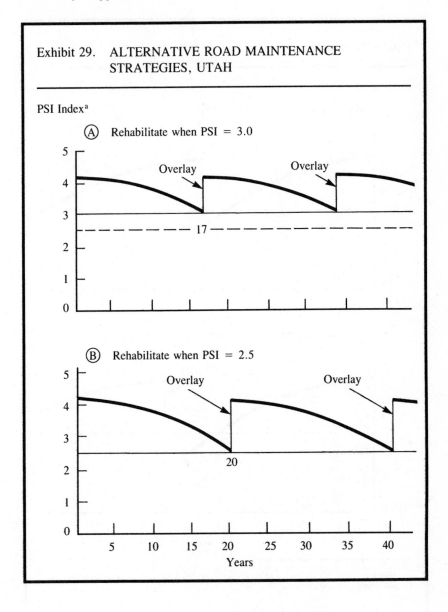

Exhibit 29.   ALTERNATIVE ROAD MAINTENANCE
STRATEGIES, UTAH

PSI Index[a]

Ⓐ   Rehabilitate when PSI = 3.0

Ⓑ   Rehabilitate when PSI = 2.5

Years

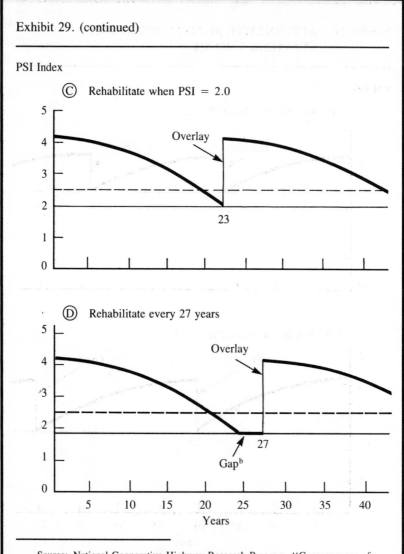

Exhibit 29. (continued)

PSI Index

ⓒ Rehabilitate when PSI = 2.0

ⓓ Rehabilitate every 27 years

Years

Source: National Cooperative Highway Research Program, "Consequences of Deferred Maintenance," Transportation Research Board, Washington, D.C., May 1979.

a. Present Serviceability Index.

b. Increased maintenance effort is required to hold the pavement at the PSI level until it is rehabilitated.

Exhibit 30.   COST COMPARISON OF DEFERRED
MAINTENANCE, UTAH

Annual Cost Summary, Utah DOT (1977)				
		Annual Costs in Millions of Dollars		
System	Strategy	Surfacing	Mainte- nance	Total
Primary	A	4.94	1.35	6.29
	B	6.44	1.59	8.03
	C	7.92	1.67	9.59
	D	8.85	1.76	10.61
Secondary	A	5.23	2.71	7.94
	B	7.78	3.17	10.95
	C	9.81	3.34	13.15
	D	10.37	3.50	13.87
Urban	A	2.53	0.82	3.35
	B	3.24	0.96	4.20
	C	3.97	1.01	4.98
	D	4.33	1.06	5.39
Total	A	12.70	4.88	17.58
	B	17.46	5.72	23.18
	C	21.70	6.02	27.72
	D	23.55	6.32	29.87

Source: D. E. Peterson, "Good Roads Cost Less" (R&D Unit, Utah Department of Transportation, October 1977).

between overlays was reduced from an average of twenty-seven to seventeen years. Even better, the average quality of the roads also increased as the interval was reduced as illustrated in exhibit 29.

Based on this analysis by Utah officials, the department recommended more frequent overlays and estimated that the added investment cost would be recovered in a little more than four years because of reduced annual costs to the state and to highway users. The Utah state legislature subsequently increased the gas tax to provide additional funds for catching up on the backlog of needed rehabilitation.

In this Utah example the decision rule for road rehabilitation is not to rehabilitate after so many years but to rehabilitate when the road condition deteriorates to the prespecified level. Depending on traffic, weather, and so on, the interval between rehabilitation efforts for any particular road segment could vary considerably.

The analysis applies to a particular road construction and repair technology. When the materials and procedures for road construction or repair change significantly, analysts should redo the plan using data from experience with the durability and costs of the new technology.

Implications

These three applications (productivity improvement, consideration of alternative service delivery approaches, and capital infrastructure decisions) are likely to be important, regular concerns for governments—at all levels. As the examples in this chapter indicate, systematic analysis of alternatives can potentially yield solid cost savings and service quality improvements.

Appendix A
Program Analysis Illustrated:
Three Case Studies

This appendix illustrates the procedures of program analysis by summarizing three actual analyses conducted jointly by personnel from the governments involved and The Urban Institute.

The three cases are not ideal program analyses. Each analysis had shortcomings, typical of those likely to be encountered by government: limited resources, limited time, and limited data. In each case, however, the topic was considered important by government officials, and each analysis affected subsequent decisions.

Each case study describes briefly the environment in which the study was made, steps taken, technical approaches used, and actual impacts of the analyses. Each has this organization:

A. Background and size of the analytic effort
B. Summary of the analysis. An approximate format is used (some modifications have been made in each case to highlight special features):
   1. Identification of objectives and evaluation criteria
   2. Examination of the magnitude of the problem
   3. Identification of options
   4. Estimation of effectiveness of each option
   5. Estimation of cost of each option
   6. Summary of findings on cost and effectiveness of the options (the analysis of neglected and dependent children also included an examination and estimate of revenue.
C. Impact of the analysis
D. Miscellaneous considerations

Two analyses were of human resource programs. All three were conducted by local governments, but the steps taken and the problems encountered should be similar in state governments. The two human resource analyses deal with services often provided by state governments.

117

Appendix A-1
Options for Improving
Short-term Care of Neglected
and Dependent Children[1]

Background and Size of the Analytic Effort

This was an analysis for Metropolitan Nashville-Davidson County, Tennessee, of alternative ways to improve the short-term care of neglected and dependent (N-D) children, from the time a petition is filed with the Juvenile Court declaring a child to be neglected and dependent until the court's disposition. The analysis was sponsored by the mayor's office of Nashville-Davidson County. The project used part-time personnel from the mayor's office and a local university, one person from the county social service agency, and two members of The Urban Institute (each half-time). In addition, throughout the analysis the mayor's fiscal administrative assistant provided informal guidance. The study was made over a period of about eight months in 1970. It required approximately two person-years of effort, with about half of this time devoted to data gathering and processing.

The problem was identified by the mayor's assistant, who felt that improvements in the existing system were needed. He had to decide in the near future whether to enlarge Richland Village, the county's children's home, where more than half of the N-D children were placed while awaiting court disposition. Personnel in the welfare agencies and in the mayor's office felt that the short-term care system was not working as it should.

The scope of the study was limited to short-term care before court disposition. It excluded care after court disposition, though the latter was also a concern of the mayor's assistant. Examining long-term care as well as short-

---

1. For a full description of the analysis, see Marvin R. Burt and Louis Blair, *Options for Improving the Care of Neglected and Dependent Children* (Washington, D.C.: The Urban Institute, 1971).

term care in any depth was felt to require more resources and time than were available for the study.[2]

Children were classified as neglected and dependent when no one was readily available to care for them properly. Frequent causes of such classification included the hospitalization of parents, severe physical abuse or neglect by parents, abandonment, incarceration of parents, and emotional difficulty. Parents, relatives, neighbors, police, welfare workers, or the children themselves could file petitions (requests for care) at the intake office of the Juvenile Court. An intake officer was on duty 24 hours a day to accept petitions. However, at the time of the study, intake officers made no attempt to determine whether the petition *should* be filed. After the petition was filed, the intake officer would place the child temporarily pending Juvenile Court disposition. If there was no clearly available and appropriate place for the child to stay (such as with relatives), the child was generally placed temporarily at Richland Village, or in an emergency foster shelter if the child was younger than three years old. After an average of two to three weeks (as found by the analysis), the child's case was heard in Juvenile Court. In 1969, N-D petitions were filed for 630 different children; 330 of them were placed temporarily at Richland Village.

Summary of the Analysis

Step 1: Identification of program objectives and evaluation criteria. The main objectives in this analysis were (1) reducing the number of children subjected to the system by screening out cases in which special care was not needed; (2) keeping the child at home or in a family environment, whenever possible, rather than in an institution, which is often traumatic; and (3) minimizing the costs of achieving these objectives.

The principal evaluation criteria were (1) the number of children named in N-D petitions, (2) the number of children kept in homelike environments rather than institutionalized, and (3) estimated program costs.

Step 2. Examination of the flow of children through the system. As in many program analyses, information readily available at the beginning was inadequate for identifying the major characteristics and effectiveness of the existing system. Intake and court records were examined for the preceding year, 1969, to determine the number of N-D petitions and the reasons for

---

2. Actually, in the analysis, a brief examination was made of longer term care options. This is described in the referenced report.

them, identify where the children were kept prior to the court hearing, and determine what the final court dispositions were. The flow diagram shown in exhibit A-1 illustrates some of the findings. The study found that 180 of the 630 children (28 percent) were brought into the system on petitions that were later withdrawn (there was no court hearing, and they returned to their homes); 332 were placed temporarily at Richland Village, and about 60 percent of these were later sent home. These findings raised substantial questions as to whether the children should have been taken from their homes in the first place. Although there was 24-hour intake of children, the existing process did not include screening and did not provide emergency services in homelike environments.

Step 3. Identification of options for improving the system's performance. Analysts identified five subprograms that were potentially feasible and worth analyzing. These options were developed on the basis of a careful assessment of needs, discussions with welfare workers, and communication with the federal government and other cities. These were:

1. *Twenty-four hour intake screening.* A Welfare worker would be on call round-the-clock to investigate each case and determine whether there were appropriate grounds for filing a petition. If so, the worker would decide how best to care for the child until court disposition.

2. *Emergency caretaker service.* An emergency caretaker would enter the child's home as a custodian, usually staying only overnight. This would be especially effective in cases of temporary abandonment, when parents were delayed in returning home.

3. *Homemaker service.* Trained homemakers, able to give many days of care, would be used to maintain children in the children's homes during the crisis period.

4. *Emergency foster homes.* Emergency foster homes would be used to maintain children in family environments when it was not feasible to keep them in their own homes prior to their Juvenile Court hearing.

5. *County children's home.* Under the existing system this was the usual destination of children for whom a petition was filed. The other options would tend to reduce the number of children sent to the home for short-term care.

Nashville already was using emergency foster homes for children younger than three years old and a small amount of homemaker service. The emergency caretaker service and the intake screening system would be completely new activities.

Exhibit A-1.   FLOW OF CHILDREN THROUGH
               NEGLECTED AND DEPENDENT SYSTEM,
               IN ONE YEAR, 1969

```
                    ┌─────────────────────┐
                    │   PETITION FILED    │
                    │  JUVENILE COURT     │
                    │       632[a]        │
                    └─────────────────────┘
                    ┌─────────────────────┐
                    │ TEMPORARY PLACEMENT │
                    │       PRIOR TO      │
                    │   COURT HEARING     │
                    └─────────────────────┘

┌──────────┐ ┌──────────┐ ┌──────────┐ ┌────────────┐ ┌────────┐
│ RICHLAND │ │ PARENTS  │ │RELATIVES │ │ DEPARTMENT │ │ OTHER  │
│ VILLAGE  │ │   100    │ │    91    │ │ OF PUBLIC  │ │   95   │
│  332[a]  │ │          │ │          │ │  WELFARE   │ │        │
│          │ │          │ │          │ │     14     │ │        │
└──────────┘ └──────────┘ └──────────┘ └────────────┘ └────────┘

              ◇ PETITION ◇
              ◇WITHDRAWN ◇  YES  ▷  RETURN HOME;
              ◇OR INFORMALLY◇  180    NO FURTHER
              ◇ DROPPED ◇             ACTION.
                  │ NO
          ┌─────────────────┐
          │    JUVENILE     │
          │  COURT HEARING  │
          │       452       │
          └─────────────────┘
                  │ YES (79)
              ◇  CASE  ◇       ┌──────────────────────┐
              ◇CONTINUED?◇────│    RETURN HOME       │
                  │ NO         │       WITH           │
                              │ GENERAL SUPERVISION   │
              ◇ LONGER ◇       │      BY DPW[b]        │
              ◇  TERM  ◇       └──────────────────────┘
              ◇PLACEMENT◇
```

┌──────────┐ ┌────────────┐ ┌──────────┐ ┌────────────┐ ┌────────┐
│ PARENTS │ │PARENTS WITH│ │RELATIVES │ │DPW[b] FOSTER│ │ OTHER │
│   54   │ │ INTENSIVE │ │   83   │ │   HOME   │ │ 83[c] │
│   │ │ SUPER-   │ │   │ │   87   │ │   │
│   │ │ VISION   │ │   │ │   │ │   │
│   │ │   66   │ │   │ │   │ │   │
└──────────┘ └────────────┘ └──────────┘ └────────────┘ └────────┘

Source: Marvin R. Burt and Louis H. Blair, *Options for Improving the Care of Neglected and Dependent Children* (Washington, D.C.: The Urban Institute, 1971), p. 33.

a. Includes two children who entered the system twice and were placed at Richland Village twice.

b. Department of Public Welfare.

c. Includes voluntary care institutions.

These options are not mutually exclusive; four combinations of them were considered as alternatives. Exhibit A-2 summarizes the four alternatives considered in the analysis. All included 24-hour screening and emergency caretaker service. Alternatives I and II combined options 1 through 4 so that all children likely to need the various services (based on the 1969 caseload) would receive them. Alternative I stressed homemaker service, and Alternative II stressed foster homes. Alternatives III and IV featured lower levels of these two services than I and II, but included substantially more services than were currently provided.

Step 4. Estimation of effectiveness of each option. The analysts made a critical assumption: that the caseload would be the same in future years as in 1969—about 630 children per year.[3]

The method for estimating the effectiveness of each alternative was based on a detailed analysis of how the 630 cases in 1969 would have been handled under each available new program, as discussed in the following paragraphs.

Expert judgment by a social worker, based on a detailed examination of each case, was used to predict the effectiveness of 24-hour screening. For each 1969 case, the social worker made a judgment as to whether the petition would have been screened out if the option examined had been in place. Estimating conservatively, the social worker found that more than half of the temporary placements could have been avoided.

The case-by-case examination also revealed that in many cases in which the petition was *not* dropped, a trained caseworker could have prevented it from being filed. Of the 630 cases examined, it was estimated that petitions could have been avoided in at least 180 and perhaps as many as 400 cases.

Similarly, for the emergency foster home, homemaker, and emergency caretaker options, the social worker made a detailed review of each of the cases from 1969. Expert judgments were made as to which cases could have been appropriately handled by each of these new options. As is often the case, the analysis indicated that in the homemaker option the returns would diminish as additional homemakers were added. Based on the timing and duration of the 275 cases suitable for homemaker services in 1969, it was estimated that 4 homemakers could have handled 34 percent of the likely cases, 15 could serve 92 percent, but 22 homemakers would be required to

---

3. With more time and resources the study might have attempted to make better estimates of future caseloads, or at least to determine how effective the given alternatives would be if the clientele mix were different than in 1969 (to help determine the sensitivity of the program decision to possible deviations from the projected client mix). With microcomputers it would be relatively easy to estimate the consequences of many such alternatives.

Exhibit A-2.   INTAKE AND EMERGENCY CARE—
                ALTERNATIVE PROGRAM COMBINATIONS

	Current Program (1969)	Alternative (change from current program)			
		I	II	III	IV
24-hour screening	No	Yes	Yes	Yes	Yes
Emergency caretaker	No	Yes	Yes	Yes	Yes
Number of emergency foster homes	2[a]	+5	+13	+5	0
Number of homemakers	13[b]	+30	+15	+4	0
Children placed at Richland Village	469[c]	−325	−325	−167	−37

Source: Marvin R. Burt and Louis H. Blair, *Options for Improving the Care of Neglected and Dependent Children* (Washington, D.C.: The Urban Institute, 1971), p. 22.

a. Used for both N-D children and non-N-D children.

b. Used only for non-N-D children.

c. Includes 137 voluntary placements where N-D petitions were not filed; many of these children would be served under Alternatives I, II, and III.

handle all the estimated cases. The additional homemakers would increase coverage by only 8 percent, and they would work only when there was a sudden influx of children needing care.

Analysts did not attempt to determine the degree and nature of the uncertainties likely in estimating the number of children flowing through the system on the effectiveness of the services. They could, for example, have used such techniques as sensitivity analysis (see chapter 7) to indicate how various changes in the number of children and the effectiveness of each sub-program would have affected the estimated overall effectiveness of each alternative. This was a shortcoming of the program analysis.

Step 5. Estimation of the costs of the various alternatives. The cost elements, such as caseworker salaries, were straightforward. The analysts assumed that personnel costs would rise by 10 percent because of increases in wages and employee benefits in the following year. In addition, the 24-hour intake screening personnel would probably incur overtime premiums. Transportation costs for many of the workers and cost of supplies needed by persons entering homes as caretakers or homemakers had to be estimated. For the emergency caretaker service, which was new to Nashville, costs were obtained for a similar service rendered in Buffalo (New York) and adjusted for the size of the Nashville program. Costs for supervisory help also were included where appropriate.

The proposed alternatives also involved *reductions* in an existing service—the Richland Village Children's Home. The analysts estimated the reduction in child-years under each option (see exhibit A-3), paying particular attention to the cost savings that would result from these reductions. The investigators examined the cost elements at Richland Village to determine which were fixed and which varied with reductions in child-years. Some costs, such as debt service for the cottages, were fixed; others, such as food and clothing, appeared to vary in direct proportion to the number of children. However, about two-thirds of the costs were identified as "semivariable," that is, they decreased with the child load, but not in direct proportion to it. These costs included mostly staffing costs, which decreased as the number of residential cottages was reduced.

Step 6. Summarization of the effectiveness and costs of the alternatives. This is illustrated in exhibit A-3. The analysts estimated costs and effectiveness both for the initial year (including a six-month startup period) and for a second year, which was assumed to have the same rate of effectiveness as the first year. All costs shown are net after the estimated cost reductions to the county children's home.

Step 7. Examination of revenue sources. As is the case of many health and welfare programs, the Nashville N-D program was financed by a complicated mixture of federal, state, and local funds. For example, the children's home was financed entirely by local funds, whereas some of the foster home program was financed under the Aid for Dependent Children (AFDC) program. Complicating the situation were changes in federal financing. Possible financing alternatives were also calculated and presented. Though the cost line in exhibit A-3 shows the combined costs to all governments, of most interest to the government undertaking the analysis is its own share. These were calculated in the analysis, and are roughly proportional to the figures shown for the totals.

Exhibit A-3.   EFFECTIVENESS AND COSTS OF SHORT TERM ALTERNATIVES

Evaluation Criteria	Alternative I		Alternative II		Alternative III		Alternative IV	
	First Year[a]	Second Year[b]	First Year[a]	Second Year[b]	First Year[a]	Second Year[b]	First Year[a]	Second Year[b]
1. Children screened out by 24-hour screening	90–200	180–400	Same as Alternative I		Same as Alternative I		90	180
2. Children avoiding institutional care through use of emergency caretaker	12–25	25–50	Same as Alternative I		Same as Alternative I		12–25	25–50
3. Children avoiding institutional care through use of emergency foster homes	36	73	89	179	36	73	0	0
4. Children avoiding institutional care through use of homemaker	126	252	73	146	47	94	0	0
5. Reduction in children placed at Richland Village[c,d]	162	325	162	325	83	167	18	37
Costs ($000)—Federal, state, and local	106	179	78	124	19	13	12	16

Source: Marvin R. Burt and Louis H. Blair, *Options for Improving the Care of Neglected and Dependent Children* (Washington, D.C.: The Urban Institute, 1971), p. 24.

a. Based on six months program development time and only six months operating time.

b. Also applies to the third and following years.

c. The 1969 cases examined indicate that most of these children would also need to be served by foster homes or homemakers. Therefore, the total number of reduced placements at Richland Village is conservatively estimated as the sum of criteria 3 and 4, not 2, 3, and 4.

d. This amounts to reductions per year starting in the second year of more than 12,400 child-days of care (a child-day is one child for one day) for alternatives I or II, 7,300 for alternative III, and 300 for alternative IV.

Step 8. Examination of implementation feasibility. The analysts considered only financial aspects of each alternative's feasibility, partly because the researchers did not sense any other major problems. Only one potential problem was noted: the possibility that many workers would not want to work late hours required by many of the options, particularly when locations were in neighborhoods considered dangerous. This could become a major problem and could increase costs by making necessary more attractive salaries or other compensation. In addition, the analysts did not examine in detail whether the cost savings estimated for the children's home would actually be realized. The reluctance of the agency to reduce its staff was a real possibility.

Impact of the Analysis

Recommendations for improved 24-hour intake screening and emergency care services were attractive not only to local officials but also to state and federal agencies that provided demonstration funds for the recommended high-option system (Alternative I). Round-the-clock intake screening combined with homemaker and emergency foster home care was put into action, and efforts were made to implement the rest of Alternative I.

Nashville began a continuing evaluation effort with the assistance of the local university. The reduction in the number of children at the county children's home took place roughly as estimated, but the added space was used for other programs rather than for cost reductions.

Miscellaneous Consideration

Throughout the study, analysts received excellent cooperation from state and county agencies. The analysis involved a number of social service and criminal justice agencies whose staff members were briefed at various points. The analysis did not threaten any significant group, and apparently most agency people felt the findings to be reasonable. The recommendations did not suggest eliminating any agencies and called for expansion of some programs and introduction of others. The reduction at the children's home was acceptable, perhaps in large part because other uses for the facilities were being contemplated. Net added costs to the local government were very small.

This study falls short of being a fully comprehensive, sophisticated analysis. For example, estimates of the number and type of children likely to come into the child care system in the future were rough. The effectiveness criteria used for evaluating options did not fully examine quality of care nor the long-term effects of short-term care, except by use of crude "proxy" measurements. No estimates of uncertainty in anticipated performance were made.

Nevertheless, this seemed to be a useful study. It appears to be well within the capacity of local governments if they supply sufficient resources and provide for a reasonably able analyst to guide the analysis.

Appendix A-2
Analysis of the Use of Police Patrol Cars by Off-Duty Patrol Officers[1]

Background and Size of Analytic Effort

In August 1969 the Indianapolis, Indiana, Police Department instituted a plan whereby a police car was assigned to each patrol officer to drive on and off duty. In the space of one month the number of patrol cars on the streets of Indianapolis quadrupled, and the rate of reported crimes and auto accidents dropped sharply. The plan received substantial publicity, and a story appeared in the February 22, 1970, issue of *Parade* magazine. Several members of the Fort Worth, Texas, City Council read the article, and asked the city manager to investigate the plan and ascertain its usefulness to Fort Worth.

The Fort Worth Research and Budget Department (RBD) undertook the study with the assistance of an Urban Institute research staff member. The RBD consisted of a full-time professional staff of nine, with a director who reported directly to the city manager. The study consumed about six person-months of effort, divided equally between The Urban Institute and the RBD. Police department personnel were not active participants in the analysis, although they provided information and reviewed findings. The study ran from March to September 1970; almost all the effort was expended in the first three months. Informal results were presented in May and results were presented formally to the city council in September. The total direct cost, which was mostly in salaries, was about $10,000. This includes both city and Urban Institute costs; the city did not pay any of the Institute's cost. There were three principal analysts, two from the Fort Worth RBD and one

---

1. For a full description of the analysis, see Fort Worth Research and Budget Department, "The Use of Police Patrol Cars by Off-Duty Patrolmen" (Fort Worth, Texas, 1970); and Donald M. Fisk, *The Indianapolis Police Fleet Plan* (Washington, D.C.: The Urban Institute, October 1970).

from The Urban Institute. Fort Worth expenditures came from existing RBD allocations. The main out-of-pocket expense to the city was for travel to Indianapolis to collect needed data.

The training and experience of the analysts varied. The two analysts from Fort Worth were candidates for the master of public administration degree. Neither had been trained in the techniques of quantitative analysis. One had conducted several analytical studies. The analyst from The Urban Institute had extensive training and experience in quantitative analysis but only limited experience in the field of public safety and no prior knowledge of Fort Worth.

Summary of the Analysis

Step 1. Identification of objectives and evaluation criteria. The analysts first prepared an "issue paper" describing the problem and identifying the evaluation criteria. The format was similar to that described in appendix B. Four evaluation criteria were singled out as potentially important and were the focus of the analysis: reduction of the number of crimes, improvements in crime clearance rates, reduction in the number of automobile accidents, and program cost. Three additional criteria were identified in the initial phases of the analysis—police morale, police public image, and citizen fear of crime. These last factors, however, were only briefly addressed in the analysis because of the difficulty of measuring the likely impact of the plan. Though data could have been obtained by surveys of police and citizens, such surveys had not been taken in Indianapolis; thus "before" and "after" comparisons were not available.

An estimate was presented for one other measure, "increased time available for patrol." While not an explicit objective of the plan, it is one that is used by police departments and is a useful proxy or surrogate measure of the plan's effect. In Indianapolis the plan permitted patrol officers to remain longer on their beats because cars did not have to be transferred at the end of each shift. In addition, servicing cars was handled by officers during off-duty hours. Similar operations were assumed for Fort Worth, and the resulting increase in time available for on-duty patrol was calculated.

Two other considerations helped set limits to the scope of the analysis. First, obtaining enough information to substantially reduce major uncertainties surrounding the plan (for example, its effect on crime rates) would have required resources that the study group lacked. This prompted the analysts to include as one alternative a Fort Worth experiment. Second, time to prepare the study was limited. The analysis began in March and the city manager called for a draft report on May 1. While not a serious problem, the Fort Worth analyst occasionally was pulled off the study to work on budget preparation problems. Thus, day-to-day budget operations sometimes interfered with the investigation and meeting the deadline, particularly in the early part of the study.

Step 2. Identification of alternatives. Analysts considered four variations of the off-duty use of patrol cars:

1. Provide a car for each city patrol officer living in the county;

2. Provide a car only for patrol officers living in the city;

3. Conduct an experiment in Fort Worth to reduce uncertainties about the plan's local impact; and

4. Await results of the plan as it was used in other jurisdictions.

Other alternatives, such as increased street lighting, additional police, and improved communications, could have been formulated to satisfy the objectives and evaluation criteria listed above. However, analyzing these alternatives was considered beyond the resources and time available. This analysis, then, should be considered a very narrowly focused study.

Step 3. Estimation of costs. Since virtually no information was available in Fort Worth on how the plan operated in Indianapolis, a program evaluation of the Indianapolis experience was chosen as the best first step. The analysis started with the formulation of a series of hypotheses as to how the plan might affect each of the objectives noted above. A trip to Indianapolis was made, and the readily available statistics were collected for each of these objectives. Because of the timing of the study only a few months of experience were available in Indianapolis; initial estimates were based on data through January 1970. These were later updated. No appreciable change in findings was noted. Particular attention was given to comparing statistics from before and after the initiation of the plan. Changes that seemed significant and attributable to the introduction of the plan in Indianapolis were used to estimate impact in Fort Worth.

Total costs were estimated for each alternative, drawing on Fort Worth and Indianapolis experiences. Such factors as initial car cost and cost per mile driven were taken from Fort Worth municipal garage statistics. Factors such as miles driven while off duty and accident rates were adapted from Indianapolis experience. Because of the uncertainty of some of the inputs, particularly for added mileage driven while off duty (paid for by the government under the plan), a number of different estimates were made using a variety of assumptions. Both capital and operating expenses were identified and estimated for each of the next six fiscal years to indicate the impact on Fort Worth's annual budget. This was important because costs tended to bunch in certain years because of the phasing of car purchases.

Step 4. Estimation of effectiveness. The analysts derived estimates for the Fort Worth fleet plan from the experience in Indianapolis. They first made estimates of the number of crimes, clearance rates, and traffic accidents that would have been expected to occur in Indianapolis if the plan had not been introduced.

They arrived at these estimates, based on historical trends, by two procedures. First, they calculated the average annual change of the historical data. This average was added to the data for the year preceding implementation of the plan to provide an estimate for 1969–70. Second, the analysts used a statistical regression analysis to determine the trend line that best fit the historical data. This line was then compared to the actual data. The significance of the differences between actual and projected data was assessed by a standard statistical test.[2]

For example, reported auto thefts declined 22 percent from the projected trend in Indianapolis. A drop of this size is unlikely to have resulted from chance factors; while it is not certain that the reduction was due to the introduction of the plan, no other factors were identified to account for the decrease.

The apparent changes in crime and traffic accidents in Indianapolis after introduction of the plan were considered to be the best available estimate of what was likely to happen to auto thefts if the plan was introduced to Fort Worth. However, there were many uncertainties in the Indianapolis figures as well as additional questions about using these projections for Fort Worth. The Fort Worth city analysts did not feel comfortable with some estimates and chose not to provide in their final report specific quantitative estimates as to how the plan would affect crime. The report also stated that no change should be expected in crimes of passion, indoor crime, and percent of crimes cleared.

Also, as noted above, an estimate was made of the increased time available for patrol. Like the Indianapolis plan, the Fort Worth operation assumed

---

2. For a further discussion of this procedure and more on its application in Indianapolis see Harry Hatry et al., *Practical Program Evaluation for State and Local Governments*, chapter 3 (Washington, D.C.: The Urban Institute, 1981). For more technical discussion of this and other programs evaluation procedures see one of the many texts on evaluation such as those cited at the beginning of chapter 5 in this volume.

that patrol officers would remain on their patrol beats longer because they did not have to transfer the cars at the end of each shift.

Step 5. Examination of implementation feasibility. An attempt was made to consider the feasibility of implementation in Fort Worth. Patrol officers were quizzed as to whether they would be interested in taking home a marked car if the plan were implemented. The city attorney was asked to comment on any legal implications.

More than 90 percent of the patrol officers indicated a desire to participate if the plan were implemented. The city attorney expressed doubts as to whether giving police officers cars for their personal use was legal under the Texas constitution; however, there was a precedent elsewhere in Texas for this type of plan.

Step 6. Summary of analysis findings.

Alternative 1—A car for each patrol officer living in the county. This option would cost approximately $900,000 the first year of operation and $400,000 each year thereafter. The Fort Worth police budget was about $5.5 million; this alternative would have increased the budget about 7 percent. It would boost the number of police cars from 102 to 307 and increase the patrol beat activity about 4 percent, or the equivalent of adding twelve full-time patrol officers. It was estimated that automobile accidents would decrease to about 10 percent below the estimated trend. Although Fort Worth analysts decided not to include any specific quantitative estimates of the impact on crime, the report noted the apparent favorable effect in Indianapolis on outside crime, particularly auto theft, and the apparent lack of effect in other crime areas.

Alternative 2—A car for each patrol officer living within the city limits. This alternative would cost about $500,000 for the first year of operation and $100,000 each year thereafter. It would boost the number of patrol cars to 240 and provide an increase of approximately 3 percent in patrol officers' time for beat activities. Whereas, alternative 1 subsidized a great deal of off-duty driving outside the city limits, this option would restrict all driving to within the city. Thus the net impact on crime and accident rates in the city would not differ much from that noted for alternative 1.

Alternative 3—An experiment with a Fort Worth-based plan. This alternative, which would attempt to resolve some of the uncertainties surrounding the effects and cost of operating a full-scale plan in Fort Worth, was estimated to cost less than $60,000 for a one-year test. Two parts of the city would be matched. Thirty cars would be provided patrol officers in one part. The other part would be used as a control group and no cars would be provided to off duty police officers living there. Results would be assessed after one year and would dictate whether a full-fledged "take-home" plan should be implemented.

Alternative 4—Continuing examination of the plan as used in other jurisdictions. Given the uncertainties associated with the plan, this alternative proposed simply following the experience in Indianapolis and elsewhere to see if strong evidence in favor of the plan became available.

Impact of the Analysis

The city manager and the police chief were kept up-to-date on the study's progress. In mid-May the city manager was given a report on the value of the fleet plan in Indianapolis and some estimates of the plan's cost if operated in Fort Worth. The manager tentatively decided to recommend against adoption in Fort Worth and so indicated informally to the City Council. At this time budget preparation began. Priorities and funds were worked out, first within City Hall and later in the Council. No one pushed for adoption of the plan. The public safety director and the chief of police had higher priorities. At the Council budget hearings the issue was not raised.

In September, when the budget had been completed, the city manager had the summary report printed and presented to the Council. The report included his recommendation that Fort Worth should continue to monitor the plan's impact in Indianapolis. The Council's action was restricted to a single member's request for a meeting with the public safety director and police chief to solicit their views. The press reported this action, including the alternatives and the city manager's recommendations. The Council did not take any further action.

Miscellaneous Considerations

The Fort Worth program analysis was conducted in a favorable environment, for the following reasons:

1. Local government officials were accessible to the analysts; the city manager, the director of research and budget, and the police chief were included periodically in discussions.

2. There was enough time to prepare a simple program analysis. The City Council raised the issue of the plan in late February, work started on the analysis in March, and a first draft was completed in May. The report was sent to the Council in September.

3. Analytical assistance was available from members of the Research and Budget staff and Urban Institute analysts. Any time budget matters interfered with the work of the Fort Worth personnel, The Urban Institute analyst picked up the slack.

4. There was a customer for the analysis. The City Council requested information on the plan, and the city manager ordered the study.

There were few advocates and little pressure to implement the plan before, during, or after the analysis. The City Council simply requested information on the plan. The police chief, who would have liked to implement the plan, placed other programs first. The city attorney objected to the plan. In addition, program costs were relatively large, and, while taxes could have been raised or other programs cut, either move would have been unpopular.[3]

The press was responsible for bringing the plan to the attention of Fort Worth decision makers. It reported on the analysis at several points, in each case, the reporting was straightforward and honest.

The technical quality of the analysis was probably adequate considering limited resources. Major failings lay in the estimation of the plan's effectiveness. While this part of the analysis is weak, it did lay out problems, uncertainties, and experience in Indianapolis. The narrow scope of the analysis, particularly the lack of comparisons with other crime or traffic control approaches, greatly limited the potential for "optimizing" the use of city funds.

The city manager had a number of comments concerning the study:

1. Had the effectiveness data been more positive he probably would have recommended a test of the plan.

2. He and the City Council preferred the presentation in the analysis of a series of alternatives with pros and cons rather than the usual limited approach.

---

3. This might be contrasted with a situation in which an evaluation is made *after* the program has been introduced. If the evaluation indicates little crime or traffic benefits, difficulties in terminating the plan could be considerable because of the foundation of a constituency for the plan—the police officers receiving the cars.

3. He viewed the study as a learning process for his staff, and he believed they benefited.

4. He recognized the risks, such as increased press coverage, that accompany this kind of analysis but did not think they should be inhibiting.

5. He did not believe that the number of person-months required for the analysis was excessive. He was willing to assign his staff for this amount of time to similar studies in the future.

6. Formal documentation was of secondary concern. His interest centered on facts he could use in formulating his own position and answering questions raised by the City Council.

7. The problem definition (issue paper) phase was quite useful.

There are several ways to look at the value of the Fort Worth analysis. One is to compare the cost of the analysis (about $10,000) with the cost of the proposed plan (alternative 2 would cost about $800,000 over the first three years plus about $100,000 annually thereafter); by this standard the analysis seems inexpensive. Another is to rely on the value judgments of the decision makers. The city manager and the director of research and budget gave a qualified yes to the question of whether the analysis was worth the effort. A third is to compare the action resulting from the analysis with what would have taken place without it. It is impossible to know what would have happened without the analysis, but the city manager and the director of research and budget suspect that the plan would have been deferred even without the study.

The analysis demonstrates the need for a nationwide clearinghouse for information on innovative local government programs. Many other cities were confronted with the problem of whether the Indianapolis plan was worthwhile. Indianapolis received more than 100 requests for information on its program. A thorough and objective evaluation document, including the cost and impact of the plan, would have been of great use and would have cut the cost and time of the Fort Worth study by one-third to one-half.

Appendix A-3
Analysis of Hard Drug Treatment Options[1]

Background and Size of Analytic Effort

This relatively complex analysis was sponsored by the County Manager's Office of Metropolitan Dade County, Florida. The analysis team consisted of members of the Community Improvement Program Office (a staff office to the county manager) and members of The Urban Institute. The team did not include representatives of any of the county's drug treatment agencies (either governmental or private); this was later to cause problems.

As often happens, the initial problem expressed by the government was somewhat vague. The county (like most metropolitan areas in the United States) had become increasingly concerned with the problem of drug abuse, particularly the abuse of "hard" drugs. Few systematic analyses of the various aspects of the drug problem were available. Judgment was therefore used to narrow the problem's focus to hard drugs, particularly heroin, and to the treatment of addicts. Drug education and other preventive measures were not included in the study, largely because the analysts believed that very little substantive data on the effectiveness of prevention activities were or could be made available during the study period with the resources available. Ways to reduce the supply of drugs were also excluded from the study.

The analysis began in July 1971. It lasted approximately one year. The final report was provided in October 1972 at a time when a recently elected Board of County Commissioners was faced with a number of questions on drug treatment programs. Approximately 2.5 person-years of effort were applied to the study. Much of this effort was extensive special data collection and processing. This part of the effort could be substantially reduced for future

---

1. For a full description of the analysis, see Marvin R. Burt et al., *Dade County Drug Abuse Treatment System Policy Analysis* (Miami, Florida: Office of the County Manager, Metropolitan Dade County, October 1972).

analyses if certain data were routinely gathered as recommended by the analysis team.

The analysis encompassed not only the county's own drug treatment programs (primarily methadone detoxification and maintenance programs with some supportive service), but also three private, residential, therapeutic community programs and a private methadone program.

By the end of the analysis, it had become clear that steps to encourage addicts to enter drug treatment programs should be an important part of future government action, and some analysis was focused on this. Early in the analysis the team came to believe that a particularly important group to consider was the addicts who were arrested, especially those incarcerated who would likely return to the use of drugs (and drug-related crimes) when released. This group includes many who commit crimes to support their drug habit.

Summary of the Analysis

Step 1: Identification of objectives and evaluation criteria for both existing programs and proposed future programs. As is usually the case, neither the county government nor those operating individual treatment programs had well-articulated objectives or criteria for evaluating their programs. It is particularly important in drug treatment to distinguish two separate objectives: (1) ridding clients of all addictive drugs and (2) reducing the amount of drug dependency and thereby increasing client self-sufficiency and reducing the number of drug-related crimes. Treatment programs using legal but still addictive drugs such as methadone might perform well on the second objective but by definition could not on the first.

Evaluation criteria were altered somewhat during the course of the study. The initial temptation was to concentrate on dropout rates (or their complement, retention rates). However, since these measures do not directly indicate the degree of subsequent drug use, the following criteria were used: (1) number of person-months free of heroin use and (2) number of persons and person-months free of all addictive drugs including methadone. Information gathered in the analysis indicated that retention in a treatment program, during which time an individual was completely or at least substantially free of drugs, was a major benefit both to the individual and to the community. Also, some dropouts seem to be at least partly rehabilitated by either the residential therapeutic communities or methadone programs. On the other hand, graduating from a treatment program does not guarantee permanent rehabilitation; many return to hard drug use.

Step 2: Identification of Alternatives. The alternatives were partly generated from initial findings of the analysis. Suggestions were made by officials of public and private drug programs as well. The wide gap between the number of persons in treatment and the estimated total number of addicts seemed to indicate the need for expansion of programs. Three alternatives to then-current program levels were considered. These included different degrees of expansion of the methadone maintenance effort, establishment of habit reduction "quick detoxification" treatment, and expansion of the various types of residential therapeutic communities.

In addition, three other major points were raised by examining the current system. (1) There did not seem to be effective provisions for giving treatment to persons passing through the criminal justice system. Thus possibilities were raised for systematic screening of persons arrested (perhaps through urinalysis) along with encouraging identified addicts to submit to treatment, perhaps in lieu of bringing cases to trial. (2) Some programs had vacancies for a number of reasons. A program may not have been known by addicts, may not have been conveniently located, or may have been known but not liked (perhaps because rules were too stringent). Possibly the number of addicts might have been overestimated. It seemed appropriate to consider options to attract clients into existing programs. Such options could be relatively inexpensive. (3) The analysis indicated that treatment programs were not as attractive to blacks or Hispanics as they were to whites. Options thus were developed to attract clients living in black and Hispanic areas of the community.

The analysis focused on near-future options and did not consider possible new treatment approaches such as drug antagonists, which at some point may substantially revise treatment procedures. Nevertheless, such considerations do suggest that program alternatives that involve large, inflexible investments should be avoided if likely technological advances would render the program obsolete. For the most part, the alternatives identified did not involve inflexible programs.

Step 3: Estimation of costs. Cost estimation for treatment expansion is not as easy as it may first appear. Cost information was available from treatment programs, but there were at least two major and common problems. First, all costs actually incurred in running a program were not charged against the program. Some costs, such as those for shared services, were charged to other programs and led to unrealistically low cost figures. Analysts had to examine the treatment program thoroughly, determine what services were provided, and check accounting records to see if these services were fully charged against the program. When services had not been adequately charged to the program, analysts had to estimate how much of the cost should be charged to the program. Some items were difficult to handle. For example, the methadone program used rehabilitation specialists whose services were shared with other programs but fully charged against the methadone program. At first the analysts did not realize the services were shared. They attributed the entire cost of the specialists to the program, greatly overestimating the per person treatment costs. Fortunately this mistake was identified by the agency during review of preliminary study findings.

Second, future costs might differ from past costs. Therapeutic communities, for example, sometimes received donated services or facilities. Such donations might not be available in the future. Some items would then have to be supported by other funds, possibly from the local government.

Step 4: Estimation of effectiveness. As usual, this was the most difficult task. It consisted of four phases: estimation of the magnitude of the problem (need assessment); a program evaluation of existing county treatment programs; a closely related collection of effectiveness information from similar programs outside Dade County; and estimation of likely effectiveness of each alternative, using program evaluation data.

a. Estimation of the magnitude of the hard drug problem in the county. An effort was made to identify the size of the gap between the capacity of existing treatment programs and apparent need, the number of addicts in the community. It is very difficult, if not impossible, to make precise estimates of the total number because addiction is generally hidden. The analysts adapted a formula employed in New York that related the number of addicts to the annual number of reported overdose deaths to provide a range of estimates. The range was between 7,000 and 12,000 addicts in the county. This range was used to help determine the amount of recommended treatment capacity.

Other indicators were also used:

1. Counts of the number of addicts who were or had been enrolled in treatment programs—there were about 1,000 to 1,500 in treatment.

2. Estimates of backlogs of applications for admittance to these programs—a wait of two to three months for admission was typical.

3. The number of deaths due to use of drugs (obtained from the county medical examiner).

4. The number of arrests on drug charges (obtained from the police department).

5. The percentage of jail inmates who were drug addicts (estimated by examining intake forms for persons admitted to the jail over a three-month period)—it appeared that at least 10 percent of the inmates were addicts.

From this information and statements obtained from treatment program records about the daily cost of drug habits, analysts made rough estimates of the total value of property stolen. Typical problems with these estimates included the difficulty in estimating how many crimes a person would have committed were he not an addict. Information also was very scarce about the proportion of drugs paid for with proceeds of crimes against property— burglary or buying and selling stolen goods—and violent crimes such as robbery, rather than by legal or less violent means such as prostitution and drug dealing.

b. Evaluation of existing county treatment programs. This was the most time-consuming part of the effort. It was first necessary to identify and describe existing drug treatment programs. This was surprisingly difficult because of the many approaches and organizations involved. The focus of the analysis eventually centered on the three major residential therapeutic communities and two methadone detoxification-maintenance programs (the county government's and a private hospital's).

A major concern in examining drug treatment programs is that some types of clients are more difficult to rehabilitate than others. Thus, data were sought on the characteristics of the clientele. Information such as length of addiction, age, sex, and race was obtained on current and former patients of each program. Because the county programs had all started in 1969 or after, there was only limited experience, particularly with graduates. Some programs keep clients eighteen months and even longer (for example, methadone maintenance programs can keep clients indefinitely).

Data on client performance while in treatment also were obtained, including evidence of drug use, arrests, dropout rates and length of time before dropout. Overall statistics were developed on retention rates, failure rates, and arrest rates. These statistics were assumed to hold in the future. The information was obtained on clients from the beginning of the treatment programs until the time of the evaluation. There was some initial reluctance on the part of programs to provide access to individual records, but with proper assurances of confidentiality, access was obtained. One program withheld records on one group of patients because of its interpretation of a federal regulation that limited access to client records of a federally funded program. With this exception, information was gathered on all clients. With a larger number of cases, it would have been more practical to sample.

An attempt was made to follow up candidates after they had left a treatment program—whether because of graduation, dropout, or discharge. Follow-up is needed in such evaluations to obtain estimates on longer term effects of treatment. Major difficulties existed. Two programs would not release names, thus preventing follow-up. As already noted, the treatment programs had not been in existence long enough to have many graduates, although they had many dropouts. In addition, it can be difficult to locate former patients. A late start for interviews in part was caused by the initial reluctance of one of the programs to have former clients interviewed (as a protection of privacy). This delay prevented a fully satisfactory number of interviews from being conducted. Recent college graduates were used as interviewers. Information was sought in particular on employment status and on the extent to which the patients had returned to drugs after leaving the program.

One major source of follow-up information was police arrest files. To avoid possible violations of confidentiality, these were checked against the names of patients by the analysis team. Use of arrest records presents a number of problems. For this analysis, only county records were examined; arrests in other jurisdictions were not covered. Not all persons arrested are guilty. Former drug addicts may be particularly likely to be arrested. Many crimes do not lead to arrest. Arrest records do, however, provide some basis for indicating subsequent criminal behavior of clients.

Analysts were inadvertently given misleading data on client characteristics from one program. The mistake was not discovered until the draft of the final report was being reviewed. This would probably not have happened had a representative of that program been an active member of the project team.

c. Development of effectiveness information from similar programs outside Dade County. Because of the newness and small size of Dade County treatment programs, the analysts also obtained information on program retention and rehabilitation rates from analogous large treatment programs in other parts of the country. These data were used both to provide benchmarks against which to evaluate the Dade County programs, as well as to provide data for projecting the performance of similar programs in Dade County. The same rates were assumed in Dade County. Programs with extensive relevant experience and data included the New York Daytop residential therapeutic community and Washington, D.C., Narcotics Treatment Agency programs. Summary evaluation data (but not individual records) were the main source of information on these programs.

Many questions arose about the usefulness of these numbers, particularly since data collection procedures varied. An attempt was made to identify differences in clientele characteristics and data collection practices that would affect comparability, such as lengthy prescreening periods before a client would be officially counted as a client (this might screen out the less motivated before the "counting" started).

d. Estimation of the likely effectiveness of each alternative. From evaluation of existing county treatment programs and from program evaluations already conducted on several programs outside of Dade County, analysts estimated likely future performance factors for each treatment mode or program. They assumed that future performance would be the same as that in the past. Considerations included dropout (or the converse, retention) rates, percent graduated as rehabilitated, likely rate of return to drug use, percent of dropouts who were partly rehabilitated, and the various costs per client-month. From these data, and from estimates of the numbers of drug abusers who would request treatment, calculations were made of the number of person-years essentially *heroin*-free, the number of clients rehabilitated (essentially free of *any* narcotics), and the program costs.

The number of person-years heroin-free was calculated for each alternative from three major components: (1) time period during which the clients were in treatment; (2) the period from successful graduation until recidivism, if any; and (3) the length of time for dropouts who nevertheless had apparently been in treatment long enough to obtain some benefit. Note, however, that society and the individual might not value these three equally. Other things being equal, it would presumably be better to be drug-free and self-sufficient in the outside community than constrained full-time to a therapeutic treatment community. In addition, it was necessary to distinguish those free of any hard drugs from those free of illicit drugs but still on some other narcotic such as methadone. The analysts did not, however, attempt to apply different values to these respective conditions.

Because there was uncertainty about the proportion of persons who could be rehabilitated, based on program evaluation findings, the final estimates of effectivness showed a range of values rather than a single figure.

Step 5: Summary of costs and effectiveness for various program combinations. The analysts produced five-year projected costs and performance for a number of combinations of treatment program expansions. This period was selected to permit sufficient time to reflect the effects of bringing in more clients and their longer-run disposition, including possible recidivism in future years. A period longer than five years was not appropriate because the long-run effect of these programs was not well known. Exhibit A-4 shows the results of these projections.

Step 6: Preparation of findings and recommendations. In addition to findings of the type noted above and shown in exhibit A-4, other recommendations also were made, as invariably occurs in analyses. These included recommendations to: (1) encourage treatment of addicts flowing through the criminal justice system, (2) attempt to discover why backlogs for certain county treatment programs were low and to make them more attractive, and (3) improve coordination among programs and consider sharing of certain activities, such as urinalysis, to reduce costs.

Impact of the Analysis

The county did not formally act on specific alternatives for expansion. The analysis itself did not make major recommendations on specific treatment programs. This occurred partly because the estimated performance and costs of the residential therapeutic centers were quite similar.

However, the analysis and its recommendations on location and intervention of addicts processed through the county jail was one of the bases for the implementation of a treatment diversion program as a substitute for prosecution.

Miscellaneous Considerations

The drug abuse problem has been of considerable concern to state and local governments throughout the country. Controversy has accompanied decisions on the particular drug treatment methods. Individual treatment program staff have felt that their approaches and clients are unique, and that they cannot and should not be compared with others. Nevertheless, a community or state with scarce resources has to make difficult choices about which programs should receive what financial support. Even rough comparisons provide decision makers with useful information on likely costs and performance.

In a complex analysis such as this one, which involves many agencies (some private), special attention should be paid to actively involving agency personnel in collecting and analyzing cost and effectiveness data. This will reduce misinterpretation of data and it should help improve the quality and credibility of the study.

Exhibit A-4. SUMMARY COMPARISON OF FIVE-YEAR ESTIMATED PERFORMANCE AND COSTS FOR THREE ALTERNATIVE PROGRAM MIXES AND CURRENT PROGRAM*

Evaluation criteria	Current program level	Added costs, services, and performance		
		Alternative 1 (high cost)	Alternative 2 (medium cost)	Alternative 3 (low cost)
Costs	$7.6 million	+$15.9 million	+$10.3 million	+$5.8 million
Individual clients served	7,500–9,000	+9,300	+7,600	+6,200
Clients rehabilitated	unknown	+ 810	+ 580	+ 380
Person-years potentially drug-free	minimum of 4,800–5,300	+9,100– +9,600	+5,900– +6,200	+3,300– +3,600
Maximum cost per person-year potentially heroin-free	$1,600	$1,700	$1,700	$1,700

145

Exhibit A-4 (continued)

Program elements	Current program level	Added costs, services, and performance		
		Alternative 1 (high cost)	Alternative 2 (medium cost)	Alternative 3 (low cost)
Methadone maintenance	3 units with total capacity of 500	+13 units with total capacity of 1,300	+8 units with total capacity of 800	+4 units with total capacity of 400
Habit reduction quick detoxification	none	+850 clients/year	+850 clients/ year	+850 clients/ year
Long-term residential therapeutic community (50 client capacity per unit)	4 units	+4 units	+3 units	+2 units
Short-term, small therapeutic residential community (20 client capacity per unit)	1 unit	+3 units	+2 units	+1 unit
Probation officers for surveillance	none	+11 units	+7 units	+4 units

Source: Marvin R. Burt et al., *Dade County Drug Abuse Treatment System Policy Analysis* (Washington, D.C.: The Urban Institute, October 1972), pp. ix–21.

*Costs and performance of each of the three alternatives are in addition to the current program. Thus if Alternative 1 were adopted, the five-year costs are estimated to be $15.9 + $7.6 = $23.5 million; the person-years potentially heroin-free 13,900–14,900; and a maximum cost per person-year potentially heroin-free $23.5 million ÷ 13,900 = $1,700.

The importance of cooperation and review by agencies affected by analysis was brought out clearly in this case. Review of early drafts of the report surfaced a number of critical issues. Had agency personnel participated as part of the analysis team, some problems might have arisen earlier and been handled better.

It would be highly desirable if service programs such as drug treatment would undergo periodic evaluation and analysis and if continuing data could be provided on cost and performance. If a similar analysis is attempted periodically, such as every two years, and if provision has been made for standardizing data collection and obtaining follow-up information, the analyses would be considerably easier to undertake and should provide estimates that are considerably more precise.

Appendix B
Illustrative Outline of an Issue Paper[1]

An issue paper is a written presentation that attempts to identify and describe the main features of a significant problem. It defines the problem, a first step in any program analysis. It attempts to develop new cost and effectiveness information as would be done in a full program analysis.

The issue paper may stand by itself as a description of a problem area and provide an improved perspective on the problem. Preferably it is used to set a framework, as the first phase of an in-depth cost-and-effectiveness analysis of a problem.

The issue paper should address the following questions:

A. *What is the problem?*

    1. What seems to be the "real" problem?

    2. What are the causes of the problem? To what extent are they known?

    3. What specific population (client) groups are affected? (If other than the general public, identify their special characteristics such as age group, race, income class, special needs, or geographical location).

    4. What is the magnitude of the problem? How widespread is it now? How large is it likely to be in the future?

---

1. Adapted from The George Washington University, State-Local Finances Project, "A First Step to Analysis: The Issue Paper." PPB Note 11 (Washington, D.C., July 1968).

B. *Objectives and evaluation criteria*

1. Toward what public objectives are or should programs for meeting the problem be directed? What are the *fundamental* purposes rather than the immediate physical outputs?

2. How can estimates of progress toward these objectives be measured? Identify appropriate evaluation criteria (measures of effectiveness). If these do not seem directly measurable, indicate proxies that might be used.

C. *Current activities and who's involved*

1. What other government agencies, sectors of the community, or other levels of government, in addition to this one, are attempting to meet the problem?

2. What programs and activities relevant to the problem are being undertaken by this government? Identify each current program and, to the extent possible, provide current costs and estimated impacts, relative to the criteria in B.2. Indicate the number in each client group identified in A.3 and those currently being served. If possible, project these into the future, based on current planning.

3. What are the existing state policies (specify statutes and executive policy) in terms of target groups, service levels and administrative approaches related to the problem.

D. *Political and Other Significant Factors*

1. Are there major political factors that seem to affect the problem?

2. Are there any unusual and significant resource or timing limitations on remedies for the problem?

3. What changing economic or social conditions are likely to substantially affect this problem or program and in what ways?

E. *Alternatives*

1. What alternative programs or activities should be considered?[2] Describe the major characteristics of each.

---

2. Though the issue paper should present an *initial* set of alternatives, this should not preclude the formulation of new alternatives as the subsequent program analysis proceeds.

Alternatives might be formulated based on one or several of the following approaches:

a. Alternative objectives—different effects to be achieved by government expenditure.

b. Alternative ways to achieve objectives—different outputs of government programs to achieve the same effects.

c. Alternative ways to carry out a program—different means of producing the same output.

d. Alternatives over time—different time spans for achieving objectives.

e. Alternatives among programs—alternatives or trade-offs among programs which have similar objectives.

f. Alternative methods of financing.

F. *Estimated Costs*

1. What cost information is currently available?

2. What information is available on the costs of the major alternatives?

3. What are the principal budget constraints and likely sources of funds?

G. *Recommendations for Follow-up*

1. What is recommended as the next step? The Issue Paper should not normally contain *program* recommendations for choices among alternatives. But it should indicate what should be done next. Recommendations as to the timing and scope of follow-on analysis, and who should do the analysis, should be made, including whether the analysis is to be of the "quick-response" or the "in-depth" type.

2. What are the major data problems likely to be associated with an in-depth analysis? How might these problems be met in the short run and the long run?

Appendix C
An Illustrative Checklist of Technical Criteria for Assessing Program Analyses

The following questions can be used as a checklist of items that should generally be found in a program analysis. This list can be used for assessing completed analyses.

Definition of Issues and Problems

1. Does the analysis clearly identify the specific problem being addressed?

2. Are the specific clientele groups that are involved explicitly identified? Are estimates made of the future size of each of these clientele groups?

3. Are appropriate evaluation criteria identified? Do these criteria cover unintended, as well as intended, effects? Do they cover negative occurrences as well as positive? If any of these effects were subsequently ignored in the analysis, were reasons given for their not being used?

4. Are estimates of *future* need provided?

Alternatives

1. Are alternatives presented?

2. If alternatives are presented, are they real alternatives and not merely added to be rejected out of hand?

3. Are the alternatives specific enough to be evaluated?

Estimating Program Costs

1. Are all appropriate costs included? Are employee benefits included as well as direct salaries?

2. Are possible costs to other departments or agencies, as well as the agency being considered, included? For example, an increased police force might lead to additional jail and court requirements.

3. Are true incremental costs identified for each alternative? For example, are fixed costs properly distinguished from variable costs?

4. Are future as well as current costs included?

5. Are imputed costs distinguished from actual cost outlays? For example, are imputed dollar values for travel time saved distinguished from actual cost outlays?

6. Are other scarce resources identified (in addition to dollars)? For example, is there likely to be a significant shortage of trained personnel required to successfully implement the proposed alternative?

Estimating Effectiveness

1. Are each of the appropriate evaluation criteria evaluated (even if only in a qualitative way) so that objectives are adequately covered? Are some objectives and evaluation criteria neglected and only data easily available used?

2. Are multiple measures of effectiveness used? Does the analysis prematurely combine measures of effectiveness into a single index of effectiveness, thereby hiding individual measures?

3. Are data on measures of effectiveness provided for each relevant population subgroup?

4. Do effectiveness estimates consider likely changes in both the mix and "difficulty" of the clients to be served and in the environment in which the program will have to operate?

Treatment of Uncertainty

1. Is there some indication of how accurate or inaccurate the key numbers and assumptions are?

2. Is some indication provided of how sensitive the study findings are to major basic assumptions?

The Time Problem

1. Are relevant future costs and benefits estimated and their time periods indicated?

2. Do estimates cover a sufficiently long period to provide a fair comparison among alternatives?

3. If discounting is used, are undiscounted figures also presented?[1]

4. If discounting is used, are the proper caveats shown to indicate the considerable technical uncertainties of any given discount rate?

Selecting the Preferred Alternatives and Solutions

1. Are the costs and effectiveness estimates compatible with each other? That is, are they based on the same assumptions and data?

2. Are the cost and effectiveness estimates of each significant alternative summarized and presented together clearly?

3. Do the analysts leave major value judgments to the political decisionmaking process?

4. If recommendations are made, do they follow from the analysis, or do they merely fall back on unsubstantiated opinions?

Implementation Feasibility

1. Does the analysis identify major potential implementation difficulties? Does it consider the effects of likely implementation problems on the costs and effectiveness of the various alternatives?

---

1. Discounting is a technique sometimes used to reflect the time value of monetary inputs. It has been used to represent the economic opportunity for removing funds from the private sector.

Documentation

1. Is the report clear, concise, understandable, and usable by a decision maker? Does it have a reasonably brief, clearcut summary?

2. Are the assumptions clearly identified in the document? Can the reader understand how the analysis used data and translated them into cost and effectiveness estimates?

3. Have all affected agencies had an opportunity to review and comment on a draft report prior to formal issuance?

Appendix D
FEASIBILITY AND EASE OF IMPLEMENTATION CRITERIA[1]

Assess each alternative in the following list of implementation criteria. Wherever possible, obtain actual factual information for the assessments (especially for the current service delivery approach). Where factual information is not available or sufficient, apply qualitative information and judgment. Judgments should focus on the *relative* merits of the alternative service delivery approaches. Evaluators should explain the rationale for their ratings. The focus of the assessment should be on likely future conditions over the next few years (for example, three to five years).

To What Extent:

1. . . . are there state *laws/statutes or regulations* that prevent or preclude this alternative for this program relating to:
     (a) procurement
     (b) personnel

2. . . . are there federal laws or regulations that make difficult the institution of this alternative for this program?

3. . . . is the option consistent with the goals and policy direction of the *agency's leadership*?

4. . . . is the option consistent with the goals and policy direction of the *governor's office*?

5. . . . is the option consistent with the goals and policy direction of the *legislature*?

---

1. Based on material prepared by The Urban Institute and the Council of State Governments (July 1987).

6. . . . is there likely to be *positive or negative reaction* by the public to such a switch? Consider media reaction. Consider both the public at large and those who are clients of the service or who are otherwise likely to be affected. Has the public indicated concern about service levels, scandals, and so forth?

7. . . . (a) Will *current personnel be inconvenienced or displaced*?
   . . . (b) Is it likely that displaced personnel can be satisfactorily relocated?
   . . . (c) Is this likely to cause employee/labor problems?

8. . . . are there likely to be important *consequences of failure*?

9. . . . are the *number and quality of needed personnel* likely to be available? (for example, is the delivery mechanism having, or likely to have, trouble obtaining or retaining staff?)

10. . . . are qualified *personnel or organizations*, such as contractors, self-help organizations, volunteers, franchises) likely to be *available*—both initially and in the future? (Applicable to non-public employee delivery options.)

11. . . . are *new facilities*, major *new equipment*, and/or *major rehabilitation* likely to be required? If so, is it likely that timely approvals for funding for these will be forthcoming?

12. . . . are government program managers and other agency *managers frustrated* in their attempts to make desired changes in the program, for instance, because of government "red tape," or if the current delivery approach is a form of private sector delivery, because of inflexibility of the private provider's personnel? For alternatives to the current service delivery mode, will government managers be likely to be more or less frustrated than at present? Consider such elements as: ability to fill vacancies, to transfer unsatisfactory employees, to get approvals for such requests as overtime, temporary employees, equipment and supply purchases, get travel funds for needed site visits, get employees needed training, get adequate management information system support, and so on.

13. . . . are *current government employees satisfied or dissatisfied* with program conditions/environment? Consider both management and non-management employees. (Applicable only to the current delivery approach.)

14. . . . does the option provide a constructive *competitive environment*? For example, for a contracting, franchise, or voucher option, are there likely to be enough real suppliers to give the government or citizens real choice of

service suppliers. For an option involving delivery by public agencies, to what extent is there motivation to improve efficiency or service quality (such as competition among managers or motivation to achieve performance targets) or is it a "monopoly" situation?

15. . . . is the agency *experienced in administering and monitoring* this type of delivery arrangement? Will additional or different staff be needed to monitor this arrangement?

16. . . . is there opportunity for *corruption*, for instance, fraud, bribes, payoffs?

17. . . . are there *interrelationships with other programs or other agencies* that would probably be affected positively or negatively and that would make implementation difficult? (Applicable only to the new delivery approaches.)

18. . . . are there substantial *fluctuations or changes in workload*—both from month to month and over various times of the day or days of the week? If so, are some options able to better respond (such as more efficiently) to such variability?

19. . . . have there been any *recent crises*, major problems, or adverse media publicity affecting the service (thus making a change in delivery approach more feasible)?

References and
Selected Bibliography

A. Principles and Techniques of Program Analysis

Burt, Martha R., *Measuring Prison Results* (Washington, D.C.: National Institute of Justice, June 1981).

Burt, Marvin R., Donald M. Fisk, and Harry P. Hatry, "Factors Affecting the Impact of Urban Policy Analysis: Ten Case Histories," Working Paper 201-3 (Washington, D.C.: The Urban Institute, July 1972).

Clark, John J., Thomas J. Hindelany, and Robert E. Pritchard, *Capital Budgeting* (Englewood Cliffs, New Jersey: Prentice-Hall, 1979).

Cook, Thomas D., and Donald T. Campbell, *Quasi-Experimentation: Design & Analysis Issues for Field Settings* (Chicago, Illinois: Rand McNally College Publishing Company, 1979).

Dorfman, Robert, editor, *Measuring Benefits of Government Investments* (Washington, D.C.: The Brookings Institution, April 1965).

Downs, Anthony, *Inside Bureaucracy* (Boston: Little, Brown and Co., 1967).

Fisher, Gene H., *Cost Considerations in Systems Analysis* (Santa Monica, California: The Rand Corporation, December 1970).

Fitz-Gibbon, C. T., and L. L. Morris, *How to Design a Program Evaluation* (Beverly Hills, California: Sage, 1978).

The George Washington University, State-Local Finances Project, "A First Step to Analysis: The Issue Paper" (Washington, D.C., July 1968).

——————, "The Role and Nature of Cost Analysis in a PPB System" (Washington, D.C., June 1968).

Gramlich, Edward M., *Benefit-Cost Analysis of Government Programs* (Englewood Cliffs, New Jersey: Prentice-Hall, 1981).

Greiner, J. M., J. R. Hall, Jr., H. P. Hatry, and P. S. Schaenman, *Monitoring the Effectiveness of State Transportation Services* (Washington, D.C.: U.S. Department of Transportation, July 1977).

Hargrove, Erwin C., "The Missing Link: The Study of Implementation" (The Urban Institute, July 1975, URI-12200).

McKean, Roland N., *Efficiency in Government Through Systems Analysis* (New York: John Wiley and Sons, Inc., April 1958).

Miles, Mathew B., and A. Michael Huberman, *Qualitative Data Analysis* (Beverly Hills, California: Sage Publications, 1984).

Millar, R., and A. Millar, editors, "Developing Client Outcome Monitoring Systems: A Guide for State and Local Social Service Agencies" (Washington, D.C.: The Urban Institute, 1981).

Miser, Hugh J., and Edward S. Quade, editors, *Handbook of Systems Analysis* (New York: North-Holland, 1985).

Mishan, E. J., *Cost-Benefit Analysis*, 3rd ed. (New York: Allen and Unwin, 1982).

Moloney, Robert M., "Needs Assessment for Human Services," in *Managing Human Services* (Washington, D.C.: International City Management Association, 1977).

Musgrave, Richard A., and Peggy B. Musgrave, *Public Finance in Theory and Practice* (McGraw-Hill, 1984).

Poister, Theodore H., *Public Program Analysis: Applied Research Methods* (Baltimore, Maryland: University Park Press, 1978).

Pressman, Jeffrey L., and Aaron B. Wildovsky, *Implementation* (Berkeley, California: University of California Press, 1973).

Quade E. S., *Analysis for Public Decisions* (New York: American Elsevier Publishing Company, 1975).

Rivlin, Alice M., *Systematic Thinking for Social Action* (Washington, D.C.: The Brookings Institution, 1971).

Reutlinger, Shlomo, *Techniques for Project Appraisal under Uncertainty* (Baltimore, Maryland: published for The World Bank by the Johns Hopkins University Press, 1970).

Riecken, H. W., and R. F. Boruch, editors, *Social Experimentation: A Method for Planning and Evaluating Social Intervention* (New York: Academic Press, 1974).

Rosenbloom, Richard S., and John R. Russell, *New Tools for Urban Management* (Cambridge, Massachusetts: Harvard University Press, 1971).

Rossi, P. H., and H. E. Freeman, *Evaluation: A Systematic Approach*, 2d ed. (Beverly Hills, California: Sage Publications, 1982).

Sackman, H., *Delphic Assessment: Expert Opinion, Forecasting, and Group Process*, R-1283-PR (Santa Monica, California: Rand Corporation, April 1974).

Schainblatt, Alfred H., *Mental Health Services: What Happens to the Clients?* (Washington, D.C.: National Institute of Justice, June 1981).

Stokey, Edith, and Richard Zeckhauser, *A Primer for Policy Analysis* (New York: W. W. Norton and Company, 1978).

Suchman, E. A., *Evaluative Research: Principles and Practice in Public Service and Social Action Programs* (New York: Russell Sage Foundation, 1967).

Summarwalla, Russy D., *Needs Assessment: The State of the Art* (Alexandria, Virginia: United Way of America, 1982).

The Urban Institute and the Council of State Governments, "Alternative Analysis: A Process for Periodic Reviews of Alternative Ways To Deliver State Services," Working Paper (Washington, D.C.: The Urban Institute, 1987).

The Urban Institute and the International City Management Association, *Measuring the Effectiveness of Basic Municipal Services: Initial Report* (Washington, D.C.: The Urban Institute, February 1974).

U.S. Department of the Interior, Bureau of Outdoor Recreation, *Assessing Public Recreation Needs* (Ann Arbor, Michigan: Department of Interior, November 1974).

U.S. Environmental Protection Agency, *Evaluation of Techniques for Cost-Benefit Analysis of Water Pollution Control Programs and Policies*. Report of the Administrator of the Environmental Protection Agency to the Congress of the United States (Washington, D.C.: U.S. Government Printing Office, 1975).

United Way of America, *COMPASS: Charting Courses for Community Caring, Tools for Collecting and Analyzing Data* (Alexandria, Virginia: United Way of America, 1987).

Weiss, C. H., *Evaluation on Research: Methods of Assessing Program Effectiveness* (Englewood Cliffs, New Jersey: Prentice-Hall, 1972).

Wildovsky, Aaron, *Speaking Truth to Power: The Art and Craft of Policy Analysis* (Boston: Little, Brown and Company, 1979).

B. Publications Containing Examples and Case Studies of Government [*Especially State and Local*] Program Analyses

Burt, Marvin R., and Louis H. Blair, *Options for Improving the Care of Neglected and Dependent Children* (Washington, D.C.: The Urban Institute, 1971).

——————— et al., "Dade County Drug Abuse Treatment System Policy Analysis" (Miami, Florida: Office of the County Manager, Metropolitan Dade County, October 1972).

Dade County Office of Productivity Management, "Library Department Productivity Analysis Study Final Report" (Dade County, Miami, Florida: May 1985).

Delaware Department of Health and Social Services, Paper on "Alternative Service Delivery," Prepared for Delaware's Governor's Management Improvement Committee, July 16, 1987.

Delaware, State of, "Report on Service Alternatives for Food Services" (Smyrna, Delaware: State of Delaware Department of Corrections, July 16, 1987).

Fisk, Donald M., *The Indianapolis Police Fleet Plan* (Washington, D.C.: The Urban Institute, October 1970).

Fort Worth Research and Budget Department, "The Use of Police Patrol Cars by Off-Duty Patrolmen" (Fort Worth, Texas: FWRBD, 1970).

Fromm, Gary, William L. Hamilton, and Diane E. Hamilton, *Federally Supported Mathematical Models*, NTIS-PB 241562 (Washington, D.C.: Data Resources, Inc., and ABT Associates, Inc., June 1974).

Hatry, Harry P., and Bruce G. Steinthal, *Guide to Selecting Maintenance Strategies for Capital Facilities* (Washington, D.C.: The Urban Institute, 1984).

Hatry, Harry P., Annie P. Millar, and James H. Evans, *Guide to Setting Priorities for Capital Investment* (Washington, D.C.: The Urban Institute Press, 1984).

Hausner, Jack, and Warren Walker, *An Analysis of the Deployment of Fire-Fighting Resources in Trenton, New Jersey* (New York: The New York City-Rand Institute, February 1975).

International City Management Association, "Applying Systems Analysis in Urban Government: Three Case Studies" (Washington, D.C.: ICMA, March 1972).

Ko, Stephen C., and Lucien Duckstein, "Cost Effectiveness Analysis of Wastewater Reuses," *Journal of the Sanitary Engineering Division*, December 1972.

Maryland, State of, "A Process for Periodic Reviews of Alternative Ways to Deliver State Services" (Annapolis, Maryland: Maryland Department of Budget and Fiscal Planning, 1987).

Metropolitan Dade County, Florida, "Metropolitan Dade County Alcoholism Treatment Policy Analysis" (Miami, Florida, April 1974).

Minnesota Department of Highways, "1976 Report and Policy for Production of Concrete Bridge Decks" (St. Paul, Minnesota: Bridge Deck Task Force, Office of Bridges and Structures, January 15, 1976).

National Cooperative Highway Research Program, "Synthesis 77: Evaluation of Pavement Maintenance Strategies" (Washington, D.C.: Transportation Research Board, September 1981).

Peterson, Dale E., "Good Roads Cost Less" (Utah Department of Transportation, R&D Unit, October 1977).

_____, "Keynote Address," in *Proceedings of the Pavement Management Workshop*, Report FHWA-TS-79-206 (Washington, D.C.: U.S. Federal Highway Administration, August 1978).

Popovich, Michael L., Lucien Duckstein, and Chester C. Kisiel, "Cost-Effectiveness Analysis of Disposal Systems," *Journal of the Environmental Engineering Division*, October 1973.

Rosenbloom, Richard S., and John R. Russell, *New Tools for Urban Management* (Cambridge, Massachusetts: Harvard University Press, 1971).

Tracy, Robert G., "Priority Assignment of Bridge Deck Repairs" (St. Paul, Minnesota: State of Minnesota Department of Transportation Research and Development Section, 1978).

——————, "Scheduling the Bridge Deck Repair Program," *Public Works* (January 1980).

The Urban Institute and the Council of State Governments, "Findings and Recommendations on a Process for the Analysis of Service Delivery Alternatives" (Wilmington, Delaware: State of Delaware Office of State Planning and Coordination, July 1987).

Walker, Warren E., "The Use of Screening in Policy Analysis," Paper P-6932 (Santa Monica, California: Rand Corporation, January 1984).

Willemain, Thomas R., "The Status of Performance Measures For Emergency Medical Services" (Cambridge, Massachusetts: Operations Research Center, Massachusetts Institute of Technology, July 1974).

Hatry, H. P., L. Blair, D. Fisk, J. Greiner, J. Hall, and P. Schaenman, *How Effective Are Your Community Services? Procedures for Monitoring the Effectiveness of Municipal Services* (Washington, D.C.: The Urban Institute, 1977).

Hatry, H. P., S. N. Clarren, T. Van Houten, J. P. Woodward, and P. A. Don Vito, *Efficiency Measurement For Local Government Services* (Washington, D.C.: The Urban Institute Press, 1979).

Hatry, Harry P., Richard E. Winnie, and Donald M. Fisk, *Practical Program Evaluation for State and Local Government Officials* (Washington, D.C.: The Urban Institute, September 1981).

Hoos, Ida R., *Systems Analysis in Public Policy: A Critique* (Berkeley, California: University of California Press, 1972).

International City Management Association, "Applying Systems Analysis in Urban Government: Three Case Studies" (Washington, D.C.: March 1972).

Kelley, Joseph T., *Costing Government Services* (Washington, D.C.: Government Finance Research Center, 1984).

Kimmel, Wayne A., "Needs Assessment: A Critical Perspective," in Ralph M. Kramer and Harry Specht, editors, *Readings in Community Organization Practice* (Englewood Cliffs, New Jersey: Prentice-Hall, 1983).

——————. "Putting Program Evaluation in Perspective for State and Local Government," Human Service Monograph 1B (Project Share, Rockville, Maryland, April 1981).

Kragh, Brenda, Ted Miller, and Kenneth Reinhart, "Accident Costs for Highway Safety Decisionmaking," *Public Roads*, vol. 50 no. 1 (June 1986).

Kraemer, Kenneth L., *A Systems Approach to Decision Making—Policy Analysis in Local Government* (Washington, D.C.: The International City Management Association, 1973).

Larson, Richard C., *Urban Policy Patrol Analysis* (Cambridge, Massachusetts: The MIT Press, 1972).

Lee, Douglas B., Jr., "Requiem for Large-Scale Models" *Journal of the American Institute of Planners*, May 1973.

Lee, Robert D., Jr., and Ronald W. Johnson, *Public Budgeting Systems* (Baltimore: University Park Press, 1973).

Lehne, Richard, and Donald M. Fisk, "The Impact of Urban Policy Analysis" *Urban Affairs Quarterly*, vol. 10, no. 2 (December 1974).

Majone, Giandomenico, and Edward S. Quade, editors, *Pitfalls of Analysis* (New York: John Wiley & Sons, 1980).

Massachusetts, State of, *Costing and Pricing Municipal Services* (Boston, Massachusetts: Commonwealth of Massachusetts Executive Office of Communities and Development, August 1982).